*Why Do I Put
So Much Pressure
on Myself?*

Why Do I Put So Much Pressure on Myself?

Confessions of a
Recovering Perfectionist

Kathy Collard Miller

SERVANT PUBLICATIONS
ANN ARBOR, MICHIGAN

Vine Books is an imprint of Servant Publications especially designed to serve
evangelical Christians.

All Scripture quotations, unless indicated, are taken from the *HOLY BIBLE, NEW
INTERNATIONAL VERSION*. © 1973, 1978, 1984 by International Bible
Society. Used by permission of Zondervan Publishing House. All rights reserved.
Scripture quotations marked NASB are from the *New American Standard Bible,*
©The Lockman Foundation 1960, 1962, 1963, 1968, 1971, 1973, 1975, 1977.
Scripture quotations identified GNB are from the *Good News Bible,* the Bible in
Today's English Version. Copyright American Bible Society, 1966, 1971, 1976.

The names and other identifying details of the people whose stories are told in this
book have been changed to protect their anonymity, unless they have granted
permission to the author and publisher to do otherwise.

Max Lucado, *On the Anvil,* copyright 1985. Used by permission of Tyndale House
Publishers, Inc. All rights reserved.
Kathy Collard Miller and D. Larry Miller, adapted from *When the Honeymoon's Over*
(Wheaton, Ill.: Harold Shaw, 1997), 19–20. Used by permission. All rights reserved
David Stoop, *Living With a Perfectionist* (Nashville, Tenn.: Nelson, 1987). Used by
permission. All rights reserved.

Published by Servant Publications
P.O. Box 8617
Ann Arbor, Michigan 48107

Cover design: Alan Furst

00 01 02 03 10 9 8 7 6 5 4 3 2 1

Printed in the United States of America
ISBN 1-56955-127-8

Cataloging-in-Publication Data on File at the Library of Congress.

Thank you,
Wes and Nancy Anderson,
for watering my spiritual sprout
with your loving care and godly example.
The fruit of your labor in my life gives glory to our Lord
and honor to your love and care.

Contents

Acknowledgments

I'm grateful to Bert Ghezzi and the Servant Publications staff for seeing the importance of my vision for this book. That vision became a powerful reality only through the careful and wise direction of my editor, Liz Heaney, who patiently helped me see below the surface and dig deeper into more fertile ground.

I'm also grateful to the many people who responded to my survey about perfectionism, both through Email and in my audiences. Your insights, anecdotes, and vulnerable sharing helped me to create a book that will benefit many.

My husband, Larry, and my children, Darcy and Mark, always contribute to every book through their support, love, and influence upon my life. Thanks for freely loving your perfectionist, wife and mom.

I'm continually amazed at the grace and mercy that my heavenly Father lavishes upon me even though I am a perfectionistic inadequate human being. Thank you, Lord, for using my efforts. May it be to your glory.

Are You a Perfectionist?

I never used to think of myself as a perfectionist.

As a teenager, I believed perfectionism was embodied in an acquaintance, Connie. A superior seamstress, Connie never allowed anything she sewed to be inferior. If something wasn't "just right," she would tear it apart and start all over again. I concluded, *I'm not a perfectionist because I'm willing to wear anything I sew!* How wrong I was!

Looking back, I can see otherwise. I'm a compulsive neatnik. Growing up, I shared a room with my sister Karen. My side was always neat—it had to be. Karen's side was always a mess, and it drove me crazy. At one point during high school, I put masking tape down the center of the room and instructed her to keep all her stuff on her side of the tape.

My constant companion was the heavy-hearted feeling of failure. Anytime I did something wrong I apologized repeatedly. My "failures" haunted me. I believed that mistakes were inexcusable and could be avoided if I would only get my act together. I thought, *If I can just figure out a way to control everything in my life, I won't feel bad about myself.*

I was easily irritated by others (*Why don't people act like they should?*); I had unrealistic expectations (*Why do I continue to struggle with the same thing over and over again?*); and I suffered from low self-esteem (*I'm not worthy of God's love; he's disappointed in me*).

These behaviors and thought patterns could have alerted me, but I succeeded in denying my perfectionism for twenty-seven years. Then, in my late twenties, God finally got my attention. By that time I'd been married to Larry for seven years and we had two children: two-year-old Darcy and a newborn, Mark. When we married, I considered Larry my Prince Charming. He had led me to the Lord, and we believed God had brought us together. I went into our marriage expecting Larry—and our marriage—to be perfect. When Larry's shining armor became not only rusty but filled with holes, I was disappointed and very angry. How *could* he be more concerned about working two jobs and a flying hobby than meeting my needs?

I tried pouting and moping and raising my voice to make Larry do what I thought he should. None of that worked, so I displaced my anger onto our toddler, who wouldn't behave perfectly either! I became increasingly angry, bitter, and despondent. Despite my efforts, no one in my life was fulfilling my expectations. Even God wasn't cooperating with my ideas of how he should instantly deliver me from my frustration. Things got so bad that I was terrified that I would kill Darcy in one of my rages. So when Larry, who is a policeman, left his off-duty revolver behind one day, I seriously considered shooting myself. Suicide seemed the only solution. But in God's grace, I didn't have the courage to use the gun that day.

Slowly, God began to show me the underlying causes of my anger and abusive responses to my loved ones. I began reading books to help me understand my feelings and behavior. Imagine my surprise when I came to a startling revelation: I am a perfectionist! I came to understand that while my perfectionism was a symptom of my deep feelings of insecurity, it was masked by my anger. God began to heal me as I asked him to help me change and give up my perfectionist thinking.

Over twenty years have passed, and I'm still working on my perfectionism! That may not be a comforting thought if you've picked up this book to "conquer" your perfectionism. The good news is that God doesn't expect you to be perfect. He wants you to grow in your faith and dependence on him. Your neediness can draw you closer to him as you depend on him. God wants you to seek his help, step by step—and that is something you *can* do!

Are You a Perfectionist?

Let me invite you to take the following quiz, which I've created to help women determine whether they are perfectionists. As you read the following statements, check any that are true of you, even if only some of the time.

1. __ Most of the time I sense God is disappointed with me.
2. __ I spend lots of energy evaluating my performance.
3. __ I tend to think in terms of "all or nothing."
4. __ I think I should have my act together by now.
5. __ My expectations tend to be unrealistic.
6. __ For me, "good" is rarely "good enough."
7. __ I often wonder why people can't get their act together.
8. __ I'm compelled to straighten out misunderstandings.
9. __ I won't begin something if there's a possibility I can't do it well.

Now, add up your check marks for your score.
Score:_____

I asked 2,600 Christian women across the country to take this quiz. You might be interested to know that the most frequently checked statement was number eight: "I'm compelled to straighten out misunderstandings." While it's good to try to clear up misunderstandings, perfectionists are compulsive about it. They feel as if they have no choice. Second was number two: "I spend lots of energy evaluating my performance." And the third was number seven: "I often wonder why other people can't get their act together."

Many of the anecdotes and comments you will read in this book were gleaned from the women who took my quiz as well as from women I interviewed personally. I asked them to tell me how they identified perfectionism in their own lives and also how they were conquering it.

When I speak on this subject the responses always vary. Some women identify with almost every statement and others with only a few. Sometimes I'll see a woman looking over at her friend's paper and elbowing her in the side, saying, "Hey, check that one! It's you all the way!" What we may not recognize in ourselves, our friends or relatives may! Many women qualify how they relate to a statement. For instance, they'll write down "1/2" or "95%." Or they'll write "sometimes" or "frequently" instead of just checking it, as I've instructed. Some women score between six and eight, yet they don't check the first statement. I always wonder how that can be, for if we truly believe God loves us unconditionally, we won't exhibit as many of the other identifying characteristics. Becoming aware and *feeling* God's unconditional love is fundamental to our healing.

Now, how about you? Which statements did you check? How many did you identify with? *If you checked three or more statements, you have perfectionist tendencies.* Someone has said: "A perfectionist is a person who takes great pains—and passes them on to others." Each of us can do that, even if we check only one statement!

But Isn't Perfectionism a Good Thing?

Perhaps you're wondering, *Is perfectionism really that bad?* I was giving a presentation about perfectionism to a secular group of businessmen and women when one man spoke up and said, "I think perfectionism is a good thing. Without it, we wouldn't have put men in space." This man believes that things must be done perfectly in order to accomplish anything. When he said that, I should have responded (perfectionists love to say "should"), "Are you saying that everything in the space program was done perfectly?" Of course, we know that's not true. At times mistakes were made and lives were lost, and yet our space program is considered successful. The astronauts and scientists involved in our space program are far from perfect, yet these men and women accomplished great things because they did their best. They performed excellently but not always perfectly.

Or perhaps you're telling yourself, "But if I don't expect my children (or my employee, my mate, my friend) to be perfect, they won't try to do a good job."

Shelly could see that attitude in her daughter's high school choir director, Mrs. Lewis. Mrs. Lewis had a reputation for her harshness with her students. She believed she could motivate her students by pointing out all the ways they could improve. Her standard was perfection, and anything less was unacceptable. At one parents' meeting, Shelly heard Mrs. Lewis quip, "Well, if I don't constantly ride the kids, how will they know to do their best?" The choir director laughed, but Shelly sat there, a slow anger rising within her. She wanted to shout, "Well, encouragement motivates them too, ya' know!"

Shelly had tried to confront Mrs. Lewis before, but the only change was that in class Mrs. Lewis picked on Shelly's daughter even more. Many of the other parents disagreed with the director's methods, but they were afraid to say anything. If they did, their children were also singled out for the brunt of Mrs. Lewis' unrealistic expectations.

When Shelly shared her story with me, I knew that Mrs. Lewis mistakenly believed that her unrealistic expectations and criticism would motivate her students to try harder. She believed she should give praise only when the choir received the highest marks at a choir competition. But Mrs. Lewis' approach backfired. Many of her students, including Shelly's daughter, frequently made mistakes out of fear. They believed they couldn't please their director; therefore they were less motivated to try. Many had even given up.

Unfortunately, many people make the same mistake as this choir director. They have confused perfection with excellence. (We'll be talking in more depth about this in chapter 7.) When we seek excellence, we feel empowered and positive about ourselves and our abilities. When we strive for perfection, the opposite is true.

The Problem With Perfectionism

In *Living With a Perfectionist,* Christian psychologist David Stoop writes: "Perfectionists are those who idealize almost everything around them. They set up standards and images for themselves and others that are impossible to meet.... Perfectionism is a subtle trap that quickly becomes a prison."[1] Author David Seamands expresses it this way: "Perfectionism is a constant and all-pervading feeling of never quite measuring up, never quite being or doing enough to please."[2] Trying to make our world, other people, and ourselves perfect leads to anxiety, depression, legalism, anger, and low self-esteem. Doesn't sound like a pleasant way to live, does it?

Many of the women I surveyed told me that perfectionism had a negative impact on their lives and relationships. Here are some of the things they said:

Beverly: "Perfectionism leads to a very lonely life. You don't want people to see that you are imperfect, so you distance yourself. It makes you crazy keeping up the charade! I praise Jesus that I don't have to live like that anymore."

Carla: "I used to think perfectionism was my strongest attribute, but now I see it as a negative. Nobody can measure up to a perfectionist's concept of right and wrong. It is a very imperfect world, so why go crazy trying to change all of it?"

Katherine: "Perfectionism stops me from trying something because I don't have confidence in the outcome. It keeps me bound to condemnation because I can't accept not becoming perfect. It's so difficult that God tells us to lead a holy life as he is holy, then says, 'Oh, by the way, this is something you can never fully attain.' Grrrrrr...."

Acccording to author Wayne Coffey, Katherine's problem, and that of many other perfectionists, stems from insecurity. According to Coffey, the perfectionist's lack of self-confidence drives her compulsiveness. He writes: "Perfectionists don't like themselves as they are, and they're sure other people won't, either. Consequently, to gain acceptance, they feel they have to perform in a perfect or nearly perfect way, thus linking their self image to their ability to do well at a given task."[3]

Other debilitating traits of perfectionism include:

- Frustration because of our inability to reach unrealistic goals
- An expectation of perfection in others
- Communicating conditional love when those expectations aren't met
- A difficult time loving self and others
- Difficulty receiving criticism—even constructive ideas— because it is perceived as an attack
- Misunderstandings and disagreements because of feeling threatened
- Defensiveness, because a perfectionist doesn't want anyone to think he or she is less than perfect
- Lack of close friendships or honest sharing because we don't want others to think less of us.

Any of these can diminish a woman's ability to love herself, to receive love (whether from God or people), and to communicate God's love toward others. One woman told me: "I feel like I drift close to God, then away, then close. This seems to happen very easily. I love it when I'm in close fellowship with God, but I pull away."

Unfortunately, not everyone sees the damage done by perfectionism. One teenager told me: "I go to school, taking the most advanced classes, expecting to get As in them. I go to a dance studio six days a week. I want and need to be the best at everything, and then I get angry if I am not. My stress level is way beyond what I should have as a sixteen-year-old, and I feel like I'm forty. At night when I lay my head on the pillow, all the faces I have seen that day yell at the mistakes I made. I think I need to be a scholar, or a professional dancer, or a winner of the Nobel Prize for literature! I once talked to a man who said that people could be great and not perfect, that they could go for an A, not an A-Plus. But I can't consider that. I cannot live without trying to be perfect."

My heart went out to that young woman. How did she get to be such a perfectionist? Was she born that way? What causes a person to become a perfectionist?

Causes of Perfectionism

While there is much that has been written about this elsewhere, let me briefly identify the primary causes of perfectionism.[4]

Abusive or alcoholic families. Homes that are abusive (either physically or sexually) often breed perfectionism in the children. Jodie is an incest victim. Her father sexually abused her from the time she was two years old until she was eight. The abuse stopped when her mother finally had the courage to confront her husband and separate from him. Unfortunately, Jodie's mother couldn't afford psychological help for her daughter.

As the years passed, Jodie's pain expressed itself through many symptoms, including perfectionism. Only a child, she believed that the bad things that had happened to her meant she was a bad person. As she matured, she tried to excel in everything in order to prove to everyone—and herself—that she wasn't really a bad person. As a result, in her school years she felt compelled to make straight As, wear only color-coordinated clothing, keep her room perfectly clean, and never become angry. Perfectionism was her way of saying, "See? I'm not really bad! I can do good things!"

But her performance (no matter how excellent it was) could not erase Jodie's feeling that she was a bad girl. It was only when she asked God to heal her wounded heart that she slowly began to replace her core belief that "If a bad thing happens to me, I must be bad."

Parents who are alcoholics are often unpredictable and have no sense of justice. As a result their children never know what to expect. Children who grow up in such homes unfortunately project their parents' (or other authority figures') unpredictable and unsafe behavior onto God. The children conclude that if a parent is unsafe, untrustworthy, or undependable, then God must be too. Since neither parents nor God can be trusted, such children begin to protect themselves by creating their own worlds, perfect worlds where they are in control.

Critical or perfectionist parents. Perfectionists often grow up in families where one or both parents are highly critical, or their own perfectionism creates expectations of their children beyond their ability to achieve them. Highly critical parents always find something they dislike about the child even when the child makes every effort to please the parent. The underlying message is that love is conditional. Therefore, the child concludes that if she can ever please her parents by doing something well enough, they'll finally be pleased with her and show her the love she craves.

Christian author and therapist Dr. Kevin Leman writes, "Parents who are always critical of their children are inflicting damage in several ways.... Such children grow up to be defeated perfectionists, always seeking perfection but knowing they'll never get there because they're stupid, lazy, crazy, bad, and all of those other things their parents told them they were."[5]

Danni's critical parents showed her conditional love. They were very religious, went to church, and had family devotions each night, but she never felt like they accepted her as she was. No matter how good she was or what she accomplished, they rarely gave her a compliment or said something positive. If she got a B in a difficult class, they asked her why she didn't get an A. If she came in second place in the cross-country race, they commented that she really could have won. When she wanted to go out with a boy who was respected by his teachers and peers, they pointed out someone else whom they considered better. Danni grew up thinking of herself as a failure. Divorced three times, she can't believe God loves her—in fact, she thinks he's punishing her for the wrong things she's done.

Joelle's parents also communicated conditional love, only more subtly, through her mom often quoting her this little poem:

> Good, better, best,
> Never let it rest
> 'Til your good gets better
> And your better is the best.

Joelle's mom may have thought she was motivating her child, but Joelle now knows that the message of this poem instilled in her the seeds of perfectionism.

Dr. Kevin Leman writes, "The mistake parents make of teaching their children that they love them only when they're good ... is called conditional love, and parents who practice it are producing within their children the belief that 'I'm loved only when I behave myself, or when I get good grades,' or whatever else it might be that Mom and Dad tie their love and approval to."[6]

Recently, I was visiting a friend who was a former schoolteacher. Her kindergarten daughter rushed in the door after school. "Mom, look at my papers," little Emily shouted. She beamed as she proudly displayed the papers before her mother.

"Oh," my friend exclaimed, "they're beautiful." Then she frowned, "But look, Emily, at this one. You didn't color inside the lines." As my friend turned back to me, she didn't notice little Emily's face fall as she walked away disheartened. That mother thought she had encouraged her daughter to do better in her work, yet I doubt Emily's heart would agree.

Of course we need to correct the behavior of our children or those we supervise, but we must carefully evaluate whether we're being unrealistic or are focusing on something that isn't important.

Temperament or personality. Although I will cover this topic in chapter 8, let me state here that a person's temperament or personality can be the source of perfectionism. Although any temperament can have perfectionist tendencies, the Analytical temperament is more prone to respond in this way if life seems out of control or if the person feels insecure or unloved. This is where my own perfectionism finds its roots.

Hang on to Hope

Hope has been an important part of my healing from perfectionism. It's easy for us to lose sight of hope when the claws of perfectionism wrap around our hearts. Yet, because of Christ, we can have hope that we can change.

My friend Liz Curtis Higgs, who is a talented humorist and author, told me, "I'm a recovering perfectionist. In my life before Christ, all of the nine statements would have been a ten on a ten scale, and what's worse, I wouldn't have seen anything wrong with it—especially the statement about why people can't get their act together. I would have thought, *What is your problem? Why can't you get your act together? You're just defective.* I wouldn't have recognized any other way to think. The passing years have helped, but most of all maturity in Christ makes the difference."

Yes, there is help for us as we "recover" from perfectionism. As we'll discover, the steps we make may be small, but they *will* make a difference.

You may have noticed that the nine statements in the quiz serve as titles of the next nine chapters in this book. Even if a particular statement doesn't apply to you, I encourage you not to skip that chapter, as each one addresses information that affects the bigger picture. Step by step, we'll take a look at the way perfectionists think and how that affects us. Then we'll discuss how to change our thinking and our behavior.

Turn the page to take the first step.

Two

Most of the Time I Sense God Is Disappointed With Me

Danielle is a forty-year-old, single professional woman who recently identified her perfectionist tendencies and their impact on her relationship with God. She's been a Christian since her early teens, but the legalistic teaching of her church confirmed the high expectations she had of herself—expectations she thought God had too. She believed if she didn't do things in a "Christian" manner, God would withhold his love and even take away her salvation.

She grew up believing that good Christians attended church at least two times a week, read the Bible every day, prayed for a period of time each day (and constantly prayed "quick" prayers), immediately confessed sin, never continued in a sin for too long (though no one could tell her what "too long" was), and tithed 10 percent of every paycheck. "I now can mentally understand that all those things are good things to do and God wants me to do those things," Danielle told me, "but emotionally I still sense I must do them to make God be pleased with me. Other Christians I've met don't seem to have a foreboding sense that God will disown them for not doing things right, but I do. Plus, I can't get over believing I'm still single because some part of my life hasn't become perfect."

When I asked Danielle more about that, she explained,

"Why else would I be forty and still single? Only when I've made everything in my life perfect will God be pleased with me enough to give me my lifelong mate. I've got to figure out what God is unhappy about so I can fix it. Then he can reward me with marriage. Is it that I'm not organized enough? Or that I don't depend on him enough? Maybe I don't pray enough or have the proper spiritual perspective on life."

When I started to say something, Danielle interrupted me and held up her hand, seemingly surrendering. "OK, I know in my head that's all incorrect, but why does my heart still think God is disappointed in me and is withholding his love and blessing?" Danielle shook her head in dismay. "I've got to do better at changing my ideas about this."

While the details may be different, many of us can relate to Danielle's deep-down feeling that God isn't happy about our continuing struggles. We may sense, as I did for many years, that God is waiting for us to become perfect before he will give us *all* of his love. Some may think that the unfortunate, unhappy things that happen to them are a sign of God's displeasure. Others may think that God is not giving them the "desires of their heart" because he is withholding his love. In big or small ways, we're not completely convinced God can really love us just the way we are.

The Myths Behind the Feeling
of Never Being Good Enough

Do you relate to these feelings and thoughts? You may not feel or think this way all the time, but to whatever degree you do, a sense that God is disappointed in you can be destructive to you—and to your relationship with him.

Let's take a closer look at the false beliefs behind those feelings.

1. *If I were a better person and Christian, I would feel God's love. I'll just try harder to get closer to God.* Many perfectionists personify the Avis rental car company's motto: "We try harder." It is our badge of honor.

Anne wrote a visual picture of this false belief. "I envision a greyhound dog forever running after that rabbit which is always just out of reach. Striving has a negative meaning for me, even striving after Jesus. The rabbit is God's love, and my spiritual running means I've got to tell people about Jesus at every opportunity. It means that if I've become proficient at praying thirty minutes a day, I'd better make it forty minutes next week. And I feel like I should attend the most difficult Bible study available in order to show God what a devoted follower I am. Then God will be fully satisfied with my demonstration of love. It's like I never quite reach the carrot dangling in front of me. God keeps moving it just a little farther beyond reach."

That's how we perfectionists think: the rabbit and the carrot are always slightly out of reach.

Jami was the oldest child in an alcoholic home. She never knew when her father might go off on another binge, sometimes leaving their home for days. In an effort to prevent his excesses, Jami did everything well, hoping for his approval. Although she wasn't responsible for his excessive drinking, she reasoned that doing things right would please him and keep him away from drinking. As a result, she worked hard to get straight As in school.

Because her father was a baseball fan, she memorized many of the baseball players' statistics and proudly repeated them to him. He seemed pleased when she did this, so when he would go off on another binge, she would conclude, "I've got to learn about more of the players." Over and over again, she tried to reach the "carrot" that would prevent her dad's drinking. "If I just keep trying everything," she reasoned, "something will make him the sober dad I want him to be."

Jamie carried her perfectionist, "try harder" viewpoint into adulthood and into her relationship with God. If God didn't answer her prayer a certain way, she concluded she needed to have her devotions more often. If a friend misunderstood her, she worried it was the result of giving up too soon when she had talked to a stranger about Christ a few days earlier. When she caught a cold, she worried there was an unconfessed sin in her life. She was convinced that if she were totally "sold out" for Jesus she would sense his love for her all the time.

You and I can suffer from similar perfectionist thinking even if we weren't raised in an alcoholic home. We may think that being involved in church every time the doors are open or that praying more will make us more holy (and as a result God will love us). We think, *If I was really dedicated to God, he would give me the power to never let a curse word slip from my lips or have mean thoughts about others.* The problem is, of course, we think our behavior is the key to God's heart. And because we believe "right" behavior equals perfection, we feel distant from God.

2. God will love me more if I sin less. Debra feels that God is punishing her and can't accept her because of wrong choices she has made. Raised by perfectionist parents who rarely gave her any praise or encouragement, Debra accepted Christ at vacation Bible school and then continued to attend that church. But when she was twelve years old, she told God she couldn't be a Christian because she couldn't stop sinning. Today, even though she's overcome a dependency on drugs and alcohol, she can't believe God can love and accept her. She's been trying to find an apartment, but when she doesn't get any response to her inquiries, she concludes, "I think God is mad at me because I rebelled against him earlier in my life. He won't let anything good happen to me until I've completely stopped hating people and doing stupid things." Debra's view of a vindictive God prevents her from receiving God's unconditional love and grace.

I've talked with many perfectionists who point to verses like Leviticus 11:44 to support this kind of thinking. It reads: "I am the Lord your God; consecrate yourselves and be holy, because I am holy." But does this verse say that it's possible for us to be sinless (holy) while living on this earth? No! While it's true that a holy God can't allow sin in his presence, it's also true that he knew we could never attain that holiness through our efforts. In fact, Scripture tells us, "If we claim to be without sin, we deceive ourselves and the truth is not in us. If we confess our sins, he is faithful and just and will forgive us our sins and purify us from all unrighteousness. If we claim we have not sinned, we make him out to be a liar and his word has no place in our lives" (1 Jn 1:8-10).

According to this text, anyone who claims to be holy is a liar! God knows we are sinners, full of imperfections and failings. That's why he sent Jesus to die on the cross! God loves us because it is his nature to love. His love is not based on who we are or what we do but on who he is!

3. I can earn God's love and approval. A third myth is the belief that we can earn his love and approval. But Isaiah 64:6 tells us, "For all of us have become like one who is unclean, and all our righteous deeds are like a filthy garment" (NASB). Moreover, Romans 3:20 explains, "By the works of the law no flesh will be justified in his sight." We can't be declared "righteous" or "good enough" by keeping the law: Yet many of us still think we can become "good enough" to earn God's love.

Shawna remembers how uncomfortable she felt when she relaxed around her home while growing up. When she was busy doing her homework, her mother would go out of her way to hug her and praise her for her hard work. But when she wanted to watch TV to unwind, her mother wouldn't approach her; in fact, she went around the house with a frown on her face. If Shawna started her homework again, she could count on her mom kissing the top of her head as she worked.

Shawna knows now that her mom was showing her conditional love. When she did what her mom valued, she was given affirmation, but when she did something else—even something innocent like watching TV or reading a novel—her mom kept her distance. Subtly, her mom was trying to control her by giving her love only when she performed according to what her mom valued.

Shawna transferred that conditional love onto her perspective about God. Unless she was doing something "spiritual," she couldn't believe God would approve. If she was reading a novel, she had an uncomfortable sense that she really should be reading the Bible. If she was talking to a friend who wasn't a Christian, she sensed she should be talking to her about Jesus. Even if she was blow-drying her hair, she would think, *I really should be memorizing a verse while I do this or else God won't be pleased with my use of the time he gives me.* For Shawna, spiritually, there couldn't be any "down time"; she had to use every moment to grow in and live out her faith.

Shawna has been learning how her mom's conditional love contributed to her unhealthy perspective of God's love. Now she's seeking God's help in changing her wrong ideas. She is learning that unconditional love—the kind God has—offers acceptance and affection, even when a child misbehaves.

Embracing God's Unconditional Love

Someone has said, "There is nothing you can do to make God love you more, and there is nothing you can do to make God love you less." God loves you just as you are. His love is complete and full. It is impossible for you to do anything that can diminish his love or increase it. Even if you could become perfect, his love couldn't increase. Psalm 89:30-33 assures us, "If his sons forsake My law, And do not walk in My judgments, If they violate My statutes, And do not keep My commandments, Then I will visit their transgression with the rod, And their iniquity with stripes. But I will not break off My lovingkindness from him, Nor deal falsely in My faithfulness" (NASB).

I became aware of God's unconditional love when I accepted Christ as my Savior at the age of eighteen. I understood for the first time that he wasn't standing up in heaven, tapping his foot, waiting for me to become perfect. Instead, he knew I couldn't become perfect and offered me the free gift of eternal life—without my earning it or deserving it.

But an even greater awareness of God's unconditional love and grace came ten years later when God began to heal me of my abusive anger. As I learned more and more about dealing with my frustrations and stopping my abusive reactions, I still wondered how God could love someone like me, a former child abuser.

During that time, I was attending monthly meetings of a Christian women's group. One day I received a call from Connie, who was on the leadership team. Connie said, "Kathy, we've enjoyed having you attend the meeting so faithfully and would like to ask you to join our leadership team."

My heart started beating faster with anticipation. I had wondered whether I could become involved at some point, but I was so unworthy of calling myself a "good" Christian, much less a leader. Even though I had stopped my abusive behavior I wondered, *Would God want to use a person like me, a person with a destructive history?*

Connie said, "We've been thinking of you for our nursery chairperson position. What would you think about that?"

I almost gasped as I heard her words. *Work in the nursery?* I knew she didn't know my background or my struggle.

She continued, "Kathy, two women are chairpersons in that area. One actually arranges for the babysitters and the other takes care of the paperwork. Why don't you pray about all this, and you can give me a call with your decision."

I agreed and we said good-bye. As I turned back to the dishes I'd been washing, the full force of her call hit me. *God is inviting me to become involved in the nursery, and I've physically abused a child. Isn't that ironic?*

I realized it was more than ironic; it was grace! *God, of all the areas that require leadership in that group, you motivated them to ask me about the area I'm most unqualified and undeserving to take.* Tears sprang into my eyes. The force of God's unconditional love and his unceasing grace flowed through my heart, wrapping it in a blanket of acceptance. "You're telling me you love me anyway, even though I've sinned so badly. Oh, thank you!" I murmured in deep gratitude.

My tears plopped into the dishwater. I wanted to yell, "I'm forgiven. I'm clean! I'm accepted! I'm useable!" I took over the responsibilities of the paperwork in the nursery, and then continued to take other leadership opportunities in that group.

That's exactly what God's unconditional love and grace are all about. Grace is a gift God extends to us. Even though we say, "Lord, I don't deserve to receive your love," he replies, "My daughter, I know that. That's why I sent Jesus to die in your place. You don't have to deserve it or earn it. Just take it as my loving favor."

We are in error if we think we can earn God's love through our own goodness. The truth is, we can never be "good enough." That was brought back to my awareness just yesterday as I sat beside a woman on a flight home from a speaking engagement. She noticed the book I was reading and commented on it, saying she loved to read spiritual books too. She explained that she enjoyed reading all sorts of "spiritual" books like New Age and other religions—even though she taught at a Catholic school. She commented, "I have a strong faith in God, but I still wonder if I'll be good enough to make it into heaven."

We talked further, and I pulled out my Bible, opening it to Titus 3:5: "He saved us, not because of righteous things we had done, but because of his mercy. He saved us through the washing of rebirth and renewal by the Holy Spirit...."

I asked her to read the verse, and when she had she looked at me, smiled, and said, "I guess I need to read my Bible. That says it all."

Yes, it does. You and I can never become perfect. That's why God sent Jesus.

He Loves Us to Show His Glory

We may not always feel God's love and grace, but we can claim it based on our position in Christ. Titus 3:7 says, "So that, having been justified by his grace, we might become heirs having the hope of eternal life." Did you catch that? We are heirs! We are princesses of the King. We were adopted into God's kingdom through Jesus.

That's grace! Grace is the opposite of perfectionism. In fact, perfectionism could be defined as "ungrace" or "disgrace."

According to Charles Swindoll, the Hebrew word for *grace* means:

> To bend, to stoop. It came to include the idea of "condescending favor".... To show grace is to extend favor or kindness to one who doesn't deserve it and can never earn it. Receiving God's acceptance by grace always stands in sharp contrast to earning it on the basis of works. Every time the thought of grace appears, there is the idea of its being undeserved. In no way is the recipient getting what he or she deserves. Favor is being extended simply out of the goodness of the heart of the giver.[1]

Many of us have trouble believing the good news that we don't have to do anything in order to be acceptable to God—except ask Jesus into our lives to cleanse us. We perfectionists want to earn rewards through our own efforts. But we begin to heal our hurting hearts when we recognize that we can never be good enough, do enough, or try hard enough to measure up. All we can do is receive God's grace and then allow his Holy Spirit to empower us to act with grace toward ourselves and others.

My friend, Sandra Wright, participates in a car pool, taking her two sons, Daniel, ten, and David, eight, and a young Jewish girl named Elizabeth to summer day camp. The three children began talking about church and Elizabeth said, "I'm Jewish. I've never been to church or read the Bible."

David spoke up and asked his mom, "Mom, is it good to be a Jew?"

Big brother Daniel spoke up and replied, "Are you kidding? Of course! They're the chosen people of God."

David turned in awe to Elizabeth and said, "You lucky cat! I wish I were one of the chosen people of God."

Later, after they'd dropped off Elizabeth at her home, Sandra explained to David and Daniel how they indeed were "lucky cats" because God had chosen them to know him through Jesus.

As believers, you and I are chosen. God's love for us has nothing to do with our feelings or whether we deserve it. Ephesians 1:11-12 assures us, "In him we were also chosen, having been predestined according to the plan of him who works out everything in conformity with the purpose of his will, in order that we, who were the first to hope in Christ, might be for the praise of his glory."

Those verses reveal that we were chosen—given God's grace—for the purpose of giving him glory. How much better could God's glory be revealed than for him to reach out in love to an undeserving person!

Once we receive that love and grace in the person of Jesus, we can claim it, whether or not we feel it. No verses in the Bible talk about basing our salvation on our feeling God's love. Instead, it is stated as a fact in Colossians 2:9-10: "For in Him all the fulness of Deity dwells in bodily form, and in Him you have been made complete, and He is the head over all rule and authority;..." (NASB). That word "complete" is the same as "perfect."

I love the story of Peter because it so clearly demonstrates God's grace. The night of Christ's death, Peter denied him three times. In the pit of depression, he went back to his old pattern of fishing, believing he was hopeless and that the dream Jesus had instilled in him of God's love had been a sham. But Jesus never withdrew his love of Peter because of his denial.

Instead, Jesus appeared to Peter in his resurrected body and dined with him. Three times Jesus asked Peter whether he loved him (see Jn 21:15-17). Peter had an opportunity to repeal his thrice-given denial through three statements of his love and devotion. God always offers hope while gently allowing us the consequences of our poor choices. I wouldn't be surprised if Peter had doubts about his love for Jesus because of his betrayal. But we know that on the beach that morning Peter made a choice to confess his love for the Master. As a result, he became a powerful preacher and apostle for Jesus' glory.

Several years ago I visited our local regional park. I had six quarters to deposit into the machine that controlled the mechanical arm blocking the entrance of the park. I deposited the six quarters and expected the mechanical arm to rise—only to realize the arm was no longer there! It had been removed! There was nothing preventing me from entering the park.

"I just wasted my six quarters," I exclaimed. "I could have gone in for free!"

We perfectionists do the same thing, don't we? We deposit our quarters of good works in an effort to earn God's love. It's as if we say:

"God, here is my 'quarter' of loving that person I hate. Do you love me now?"

Or, "Here, God, is my 'quarter' of having my devotional time today. Do you love me now?"

Or, "Here is my 'quarter' of serving in the nursery even though I would rather go to the service. Do you love me now?"

We put in our quarters, hoping to gain God's approval and enter into his love. What we fail to realize is that nothing stands in the way of God's love for us. Jesus died on the cross in our place and has shattered the only obstacle—sin. The price has been paid. Instead of putting in the quarters, we can move forward into experiencing God's love.

Certainly, God wants our obedience. He wants us to love others, to have our quiet times with him, and to serve in our churches. But those things should be done out of our love for him, not as a means of earning his love and approval.

We can experience that grace-filled love even when we don't have any quarters to put into the machine of performance. That was the experience of Karla Faye Tucker, who in February of 1998, was the hottest topic on television and talk radio. As she waited on death row in Huntsville, Texas, to see whether the governor would pardon her, she expressed her Christian faith in her assurance that she would be in heaven if executed—even though she had been a pickax murderer.

As I listened one evening to a radio talk show on the

subject, one woman said, "Those Christians should be more selective about who they admit into their kingdom."

I smiled. That woman didn't understand how God "admits" sinners into his kingdom. Every single one of us deserves the execution Karla Faye Tucker received on February 3, 1998. None of us are *selected* into heaven based on our worthiness. We are *offered* God's unconditional grace and forgiveness, and a home in heaven, based on Jesus' dying in our place. Karla Faye accepted that grace, even though she didn't deserve it. She had no quarters to give.

Are you willing to stop trying to earn God's love? He wants you to know his incredible, unconditional love. He loves you and wants only the best for you. Go forward into his love. Nothing is blocking you.

Three

Three

*I'm Always Evaluating
My Performance*

This morning when I woke up, I was excited to begin the day. I looked down and saw that around my neck hung a placard with my name beautifully printed in calligraphy. The placard represented how I was feeling about myself.

But as I was cooking oatmeal for breakfast, it boiled over. *What a mess. How stupid! I should have been paying more attention,* I told myself. As soon as those thoughts formed, I heard a ripping sound. I looked down and my placard had a tear. *No big deal,* I thought.

Later at a church meeting that morning, one of my friends commented, "You're not going to fix that lemon gelatin salad for the potluck Saturday, are you?" I was momentarily stunned but quickly revised the menu I had planned and said, "No, I'm going to bring a … a … tossed green salad." Another friend interrupted us, and I walked away feeling angry and perplexed. *What's wrong with my lemon gelatin salad? I always thought it was good. I must be wrong. I guess I'm not a good cook, after all.* Again, I heard a ripping sound.

At lunchtime, Darcy and Mark got on my nerves and I yelled at them. I calmed down but was filled with regret. *Why do I always yell at the kids? I'm never patient! I'm a terrible*

39

mother. My kids will most likely grow up to be juvenile delinquents because of me. R-r-r-r-rip. I looked down and saw that the lower right corner of the poster had fallen to the ground.

That afternoon I received a call from a friend who needed a ride to the doctor's office. She said it was an emergency and no one else was available. I was happy to drive her, but it took longer than expected, and I got home just before Larry. I told him dinner would be late and he got irritated. I rushed around trying to appease him. *I can't do anything right. I deserve his anger. I should have planned better.* R-r-r-r-rip.

By the time I crawled into bed, my placard was worn and frayed—nothing remained of its original beauty. I cried myself to sleep feeling frustrated and depressed.

Does this story sound farfetched? Not to me. Like most perfectionists, I used to evaluate everything I did, and I focused on what I did wrong rather than what I did right. I often went to sleep feeling like a failure and determined to do better the next day.

Consider what other perfectionists have told me:

- "I've started a new part-time seasonal job. It has been a challenge for me not to rehearse what I said and did the entire workday after I get home. It makes me lose sleep, and I get very anxious."

- "Some of my friends and I joke about having 'The Imposter Syndrome.' We are all successful in our careers, and we all worry that our success is a fluke and that we are not nearly as competent as people think. Our big fear is that one of these days, someone will look at us carefully and see our flaws and reveal the truth to the rest of the world."

- "Every day I come home and go over everything I did or said to others. Did I talk too much at the meeting? Are people talking about me behind my back? What do others think of me? I'm constantly trying to monitor what others expect of me and pour my energy into meeting (or exceeding) those expectations."

- "Some days I wake up and all I can think about is what a bad mom I was the day before—maybe I yelled at the kids for just being kids, or I got home from shopping too late and brought home dinner from Burger King. I want to be a good mom, but I feel like I'm always failing my family. I tell myself I'll do better, that I'll learn from my mistakes and I'm sure I do, but it doesn't take away my anxiety. My husband tells me I'm a good mom and to stop evaluating everything I do, but it's so hard."

Each of the above is an example of what psychologist David Stoop calls negative self-talk. In *Self-Talk: Key to Personal Growth*, Stoop says that negative self-talk often makes us feel like failures, like we never measure up.

Our Own Worst Critic

I often compare the mind to a tape recorder. Our brains record our experiences onto tapes and we replay those tapes constantly. This is especially true of the perfectionist. Since she is her own worst critic, the perfectionist replays tapes labeled "poor response" and "didn't do the right thing" and "failed at that too." She bases her worth on how she performs, and her self-talk tells her she's not worth much.

Three words characterize negative self-talk:

- I *should* have done it differently...
- I *would* have done it differently if only ...
- I *could* have done it better if...

This has been called "the tyranny of the oughts." Such thinking burdens a person with condemnation and regret, destroying her confidence in herself and in God's love for her. These thoughts can be crippling, stripping a woman of hope and insight for the future. If we constantly focus our thoughts on our behavior rather than on who we are in Christ, we'll always come up wanting. Just ask Susan.

When Susan was a child, her mother repeatedly told her she was stupid and ugly and would never succeed. When Susan did something wrong, her mother instructed everyone in the family not to speak to her. Only after she apologized could she participate in the family's activities. As a result, Susan believed she was lovable and acceptable only when she obeyed and was good.

Now that she has her own family, Susan still has trouble looking people in the eye and believing that anyone wants to be her friend. When she attempts a new project, something inside her says, *It'll never work out; I'll fail for sure.* When she meets someone at church, she leaves as quickly as possible, thinking, *They won't like me. No one would want to get to know me better.*

When Susan's children cry or have temper tantrums, she thinks, *See what a terrible mother I am? I can't even make my children happy.*

Laura, Susan's two-year-old, repeatedly has toilet training

accidents. Susan reacts in rage each time. In the back of her mind she tells herself, *I know Laura can go potty in the toilet. She's not cooperating just to show me she hates me.*

Even though she is an adult, Susan is still playing the tapes her brain recorded when she was a child. Her life illustrates Proverbs 23:7: "For as he thinks within himself, so he is" (NASB). Until she begins to think differently about herself, she'll never succeed, have close friendships, or control her outbursts.

Self-deprecating thoughts often seem reasonable and accurate at the moment. We may think *I can't do anything right* immediately after making a mistake, but we fail to recall that the day before we succeeded in a difficult project, perhaps even more difficult than the one at which we just "failed."

Susan needs to learn to take her thoughts captive.

Taking Your Thoughts Captive

I've learned that the best way to combat negative self-talk is to apply the wisdom found in 2 Corinthians 10:5b: "taking every thought captive to the obedience of Christ" (NASB).

In the past I always believed that as soon as I would think a thought, it was a part of me. If that thought was negative or condemning, I believed I had sinned just by thinking it. But this verse indicates otherwise. It says that our thoughts are like arrows that fly into our minds. Each time an arrow enters our minds, we can grasp it and ask, "Is this the way God wants me to think?" According to this command, we have the power to take each thought captive, examine it, cast away the thoughts that do not honor God, and accept only those that are godly and mature.

As we take our thoughts "captive to Christ," we align our thinking with God's Word and look at our circumstances the way God does. By correcting negative self-talk, we are able to accept and focus on this truth: *Because I am made in God's image, I am a valuable and worthy person. My worth and significance are not attached to my achievements and successes. Even when I fail, God still loves and values me. He will never give up on me.*

Scripture gives us two keys to taking our self-talk captive:

1. *Think the truth about ourselves.* Romans 12:3 tells us to "think so as to have sound judgment." God wants us to think truthfully about ourselves, to acknowledge our weaknesses and our strengths. Most of all, he wants us to believe we have value as his child and power through the Holy Spirit. Therefore, we can think: *I will succeed in God's power. I am valuable as a human being, created by God. I can be a good friend, someone people like to be around.*

2. *"Fill your minds with those things that are good and that deserve praise: things that are true, noble, right, pure, lovely, and honorable"* (Phil 4:8, GNB). It takes time and discipline to change our thinking and align it with God's Word. It's not realistic to think, *OK, I'm never going to hate myself again,* or *I'm never going to think I'm a bad mother again.* It may take a long time—years—to change the tapes running in your mind. If, as a child, you repeatedly said to yourself, "I'm no good," or "No one loves me," it's going to take extensive reprogramming to wipe out all that negative information. But it can be done!

Replace Negative Self-Talk With the Truth of Scripture

Not only can we take every thought captive, and thereby reject the lies of negative self-talk, we can also replace our negative tapes with Scripture. This is the most powerful way to take our thoughts "captive." Second Timothy 3:16-17 tells us, "All Scripture is inspired by God and profitable for teaching, for reproof, for correction, for training in righteousness; that the man of God may be adequate, equipped for every good work" (NASB). As we meditate on a verse to replace our negative self-talk, we will overcome our perfectionist thinking.

Here are some examples of how we can do that:

Negative Self-Talk	Corrective Self-Talk	Accompanying Scripture
I gossiped after I said I never would again. I'm just hopeless.	I made a mistake, but it's not the end of the world. I'll ask God's forgiveness and forgive myself.	"If we confess our sins, he is faithful and righteous to forgive our sins and to cleanse us from all unrighteousness" (1 Jn 1:9 NASB).
I never have been good at speaking before groups. I might as well give up my job.	I didn't do as well this time, but next time I'll do better. I've learned something from this.	"I can do all things through Christ who strengthens me" (Phil. 4:13 NASB).

Negative Self-Talk	Corrective Self-Talk	Accompanying Scripture
If I don't hurry, I'm going to blow this whole thing.	I'm not going to get anxious. I'll do my best and not rush.	"Be anxious for nothing, but in everything by prayer and supplication with thanksgiving let your requests be made know to God. And the peace of God, which surpasses all comprehension, shall guard your hearts and your minds in Christ Jesus" (Phil 4:6-7)NASB.
If I were a better mother, my child wouldn't act this way.	My child isn't perfect, but I've done the best I know how.	"But everyone will die for his own iniquities; each man who eats the sour grapes, his teeth will be set on edge" (Jer 31:30)NASB.
You're never going to be perfect.	Only Jesus is perfect. God just wants me to keep growing closer to him.	"For I am confident of this very thing, that he who began a good work in you will perfect it until the day of Christ Jesus" (Phil 1:6).
I hate myself.	God loves me and I love myself. How can I not love something God made and loves?	"Since you are precious in my sight, since you are honored and I love you, I will give other men in your place and other peoples in exchange for your life (Is 43:4)NASB.

Negative Self-Talk	Corrective Self-Talk	Accompanying Scripture
I'll never conquer this sin.	It may be taking me a while to get victory over this, but God knows he'll do it in his power.	"Therefore the Lord longs to be gracious to you, and therefore he waits on high to have compassion on you" (Is 30:18a)NASB.
I'm so worried about ...	God is in control. I'm going to trust him.	"Do not fear, for I am with you; Do not anxiously look about you, for I am your God. I will strengthen you, surely I will help you. Surely I will uphold you with My righteous right hand" (Is 41:10)NASB.

Prompters for Change

To break the habit of negative self-talk, we need "prompters" or signals to remind us to stop and notice how we've been thinking. Here are some ideas I've found helpful:

1. On several pieces of paper write down a negative phrase that you often tell yourself. Beside it write out a Scripture verse that gives God's perspective on the matter. Post these throughout your home and office so you will be reminded of how God wants you to think about yourself.

2. Identify an external stimulus that triggers attention to what you've been thinking about yourself. For instance, every time you change the baby, ask yourself, "What have I been saying to myself in the last couple of minutes?" Or if you have a watch with an alarm, set it to go off every hour or half hour to call your attention to your self-talk. Or every time your child asks for something to eat or drink, or when the phone rings, or the clock chimes—just choose something that happens regularly and frequently and use it to correct any demeaning thoughts.

3. Wear a rubber band around your wrist and "snap" yourself every time you allow something negative to take hold of your mind. When I speak to audiences about perfectionism, I provide a rubber band for each person and suggest they snap themselves when they have a self-deprecating thought. I also tell them, "If you hear someone else verbalizing negative self-talk, you have permission to snap that person's rubber band." The response of the group is immediate as they recognize how they can help each other. Throughout the retreat, women are laughing and snapping their own rubber bands and those of others around them. Many report they had no idea how often they think negatively about themselves. From that beginning, they are empowered to correct their perfectionist thinking.

During a recent women's retreat, I shared these principles and distributed rubber bands. A month later I received a letter from one woman who had attended that weekend. She wrote, "Kathy, I can't believe how much wearing the rubber band has made a difference in my thinking and behavior. Every time I start to tear myself down, I see my rubber band on my wrist and correct my thinking to believe the truth: that in spite of a troubled childhood and believing I was worthless, I am a beloved child of God. God will never stop loving me. I don't know how much longer I will be wearing my rubber band, but I'm going to wear it as long as I need to."

Begin Today

Once, after I had spoken to a group of young mothers, one of the women, Vicki, asked if she could talk with me privately. We sat alone and she poured out her heart about her twelve-year-old daughter, Cassie. Vicki described Cassie as a strong-willed child who demanded more from Vicki than she could give. As a result she was often frustrated and angry at Cassie.

Vicki moaned, "I should have valued my time with Cassie when she was younger. If only I had paid more attention to her, I would have a better relationship with her now. Before my husband and I divorced, I concentrated on 'fixing' my husband and didn't give Cassie the love she needed. When my husband and I decided to divorce, I had to go back to work full-time, and I had even less time to give to her.

"I know I shouldn't give excuses. It's just that I'm terrified that my lack of attention has made her hate me. I'm sure she's going to be rebellious in her teens. What if she starts taking drugs or gets pregnant? If she does, it's going to be my fault."

From Vicki's description, I envisioned Cassie as an out-of-control preteen, but when I began asking Vicki some questions, I was surprised at her answers.

"Vicki, how is your relationship with Cassie right now?"

She paused to think. "Well, actually, pretty good. I'm shocked sometimes."

"Does she listen to you fairly well?"

Another thoughtful pause. "Yeah, right now she does."

I laughed and Vicki stared at me, puzzled. "But you indicated you don't have a good relationship with her."

"No, I just think it could be better than it is now," she explained.

"OK, now I understand. Here's what I'm sensing. See what you think. You keep evaluating everything you've done in the past so that you're not appreciating how good you have it right now."

Vicki's eyes widened.

After waiting for my words to sink in, I said, "Do you feel like sometimes a tape is playing in your mind, rehearsing all the wrong things you've done to Cassie?"

"Oh, yes, I do. I just keep thinking over and over again how I've blown it. I don't deserve to have Cassie come out right as an adult. What should I do?"

"All your efforts to judge yourself from the past are preventing you from giving her the attention she needs right now—the very thing you're regretting about her childhood."

Vicki's eyes widened more. Her voice was almost a whisper. "You're right."

"You can't change the past or the future, but you can change right now."

Vicki brushed tears from her eyes. "I'm going to do that. We do have a good relationship right now. I'm going to capitalize on that and not let my past performance spoil the future."

We hugged and then prayed.

I heard from Vicki later, and she has begun changing those negative tapes playing in her mind. I know you can do the same. You will find the same transforming power over your perfectionist thinking by "taking every thought captive to the obedience of Christ." Be aware of your "shoulds, coulds, and woulds"; be sure to confess any sin, as needed; then go on knowing you are a confident woman—and act like it!

Four

I Think in Terms of "All or Nothing"

"I can't begin another project until my desk is completely clean from the old one."

* * *

"It's hard for me to value a short amount of time with the Lord. I keep waiting until my schedule opens up so I can have an hour."

* * *

"If my kids load the dishwasher but leave one dish in the sink, I can't tell them they did a good job. I get angry about the one dish."

* * *

"When I play on my soccer team, I think I have to make three goals in order to give myself credit for a job well done—no matter how difficult the opposing team is."

* * *

Can you relate to any of these "all or nothing" statements? If you can, you're not alone. Perfectionists give credit or praise only when something is done completely and perfectly. To the perfectionist, a person's best effort is not sufficient. Nothing less than perfection is acceptable. Such thinking is that of a harsh taskmaster.

Let me give you an example. Recently I made a commitment to eat healthfully all day. I did well until that evening. Larry took me out to dinner and I couldn't resist eating a piece of chocolate raspberry cheesecake. As we drove home from the restaurant, I began reprimanding myself for my "slip." *I blew it! I did so well all day. Why did you do that, Kathy?* I asked myself over and over again. Can you see the "all or nothing" thinking reflected in my negative self-talk?

But then I caught myself. (I should have been wearing my rubber band so I could snap it!) *Kathy, you didn't do it 100 percent but you had a good day. It was an 80 percent day, maybe even 90 percent. Why not give the Lord credit for the power he gave you?* In that moment, I was able to correct what Christian psychologist Dr. David Stoop calls "dichotomous thinking." He says:

> This style of thinking breaks everything into dichotomies, where everything is either in one class or in its opposite.... "Either I'm a straight-A student or I'm too dumb to learn" or "either I'm a good mother or I'm a bad mother" or "either I'm popular or I'm a nerd" or "either I'm a great artist or I'm wasting my time even trying." In this process, perfectionists develop an absolutistic attitude about themselves, believing that it is unacceptable to have any degree of some "negative" quality, such as jealousy, anger, or selfishness, or any kind of "negative" behaviors.[1]

According to Dr. Stoop, dichotomous thinking reveals itself through the use of "absolute words." We perfectionists say things like:

- "I've *never* been able to reach out to people."
- "I'm *always* disorganized."
- "I can't *ever* get everything done that I should."
- "I forget names *all the time*."
- "I'm *constantly* burning the roast."

Do you see the pattern? The words *never, always, ever, all the time,* and *constantly* reflect "all or nothing" thinking: *If I can't do it 100 percent correctly, then I might as well give up because less than that just doesn't count.* If we don't think we've performed perfectly, we can't accept a compliment. If the casserole turns out well but the vegetables are undercooked, we consider the meal a failure. If our husband remembered our birthday a day late, we think he doesn't love us. We only notice that the glass is half empty; we never see it as half full. In fact, we look at the glass and see it dry!

If left unchallenged, this mind-set can be debilitating. Just ask Allisa. She home-schooled her two daughters and wanted to do it perfectly. But her unrealistic expectations drove her into deep depression. Nothing could be done halfheartedly or less than 100 percent correctly. She kept meticulous lesson plans, often staying up until 2 A.M. to study and prepare for the lessons. She believed her children's achievements reflected her own personal value.

She explained, "My older daughter and I are poor spellers, so I insisted we look up every single word in the dictionary before a written paper, even a worksheet, could be considered finished. I couldn't be flexible. If an opportunity for the girls came up for them to go on an unscheduled field trip with another group of home-schooled children, I couldn't let my girls go unless we had completed everything I had planned.

Even if the field trip would enhance their learning, my plan was more important. If something got done even 90 percent, I believed I had failed that day."

Allisa's unrealistic expectations began to take their toll. She constantly compared herself with other moms who home-schooled and always felt she never measured up to them.

Eight years after she began home-schooling her daughters, Allisa became clinically depressed. Exhaustion and stress had attacked her body and created a chemical imbalance. She had panic attacks and couldn't function. Even simple decisions, such as what vegetable to have for dinner, overwhelmed her. She tried to push away her friends, not wanting them to know she wasn't coping. She got to the point where she couldn't even prepare her lessons and teach the girls. Ironically, all her efforts to do everything perfectly had taken away the very thing she wanted: to help her children succeed.

She felt defeated and hopeless. "I never had a good day. I couldn't sleep; I lost weight; I would have panic attacks that went on for days. I took tranquilizers so that I could accomplish just a little for a few hours. I didn't even want to live anymore; I felt like such a failure."

But in time Allisa experienced God's healing. Through the help of a counselor, she discovered the reasons for her panic attacks and began to identify her perfectionism. She recognized that her "all or nothing" thinking had caused her to be obsessive about home-schooling—to the exclusion of other things. Eventually, she learned to teach her daughters with more flexibility and even to include fun! She also allowed her friends to know she couldn't be perfect. When they responded with compassion, calling her to tell her they were praying, she felt hopeful. Her fears of being considered a failure as a mother and home-schooler were alleviated through their unconditional love and acceptance.

Today, Allisa says, "The home-schooling didn't cause my clinical depression. Home-schooling was simply the vehicle through which my perfectionist tendencies became out of balance."

"But I can see that it wasn't all bad. Our daughters are doing well in school now. My fourteen-year-old daughter has a good grasp of Scripture and truly loves the Lord. My eleven-year-old keeps good prayer lists and enjoys contemporary Christian music. God is good—all the time."

Allisa has learned that even in the midst of negative circumstances, she can focus on the good things. Until she took steps to overcome her perfectionism, she was unable to do this. Now she gives herself credit for the good influence she *did* have on her girls, even if it wasn't total.

Raising the Bar Higher and Higher

Sadly, perfectionists are rarely satisfied. Even if we do something well, we always think of ways we could have done it better. Dr. Kevin Leman calls this the "high jump bar of life."[2] We perfectionists are like high jumpers who, once we get over the bar at eight feet, feel compelled to raise it to eight-and-a-half feet. Even if we can succeed at something, we can't accept that as success. We have to do it even better ... and better ... and better.

Let me tell you what I mean. Eileen loves to entertain for the holidays. She goes all out, with both the food and the decorations. One year for her husband's office Christmas party, she cooked and served prime rib with lots of different salads, breads, and desserts. She received numerous compliments on the delicious food and beautiful table decorations. So she decided to make the dinner *really* special the next year.

The next year Eileen cooked a pig in a pit in their backyard! Plus, she prepared even more gourmet dishes, requiring more of her time. But even then she wasn't satisfied with the compliments. She started thinking, *Well, if I can do that, then what can I do next year to really make people say "Wow!"*

Later, Eileen shared her thoughts with me. "I didn't even realize I was trying to earn approval with my efforts. I guess I was thinking that *if* and *when* I made everything perfect, then I'd get the love I needed."

Eileen raised the bar higher, always thinking that would earn her the love and acceptance for which she longed. Sadly, though, when we don't or can't believe and receive the unconditional love of God, we try to get it from other sources—such as accomplishments and people's approval. But even then, it's never enough! Even if we are successful, we continue to think of ways we can improve what we've done!

God's Perspective

Many perfectionists believe God has an "all or nothing" attitude toward our behavior. Consequently we conclude, "Since I can't spend an hour of quiet time with God, I won't spend any time, even though I have ten minutes right now." We fear entering God's presence because we're ashamed we haven't done *enough* or spent *enough* time with him to earn an audience. But is this consistent with Scripture? If it were—if God truly expected us to be perfect in every way—God would not be pleased with *any* of us, at *any* time, for we all fall short, no matter what we do!

Scripture portrays a different story. The Bible records God's commendations of many men and women who were far from perfect. Hebrews 11 is the Christian's Hall of Fame—it names people whom God says showed great faith. Abraham is listed in this passage. "By faith Abraham, even though he was past age—and Sarah herself was barren—was enabled to become a father because he considered him faithful who had made the promise" (Heb 11:11). This is astounding when you consider how Abraham and Sarah grew tired of waiting for God to fulfill his promise of a son and took matters into their own hands. Sarah convinced Abraham to impregnate her servant, Hagar, so he would have a son. And he did! Yet, God declares that Abraham and Sarah showed great faith that God would fulfill his promise. Doesn't sound like an "all or nothing" attitude to me. If God were a perfectionist, he wouldn't have given them any credit at all.

Similarly, God would not have praised Moses, either, but in Hebrews 11:24-28, Moses is praised for:

- Refusing to be called the son of Pharaoh's daughter
- Being willing to endure ill treatment with the Israelites
- Considering a spiritual life more important than the treasures of Egypt
- Leading the Israelites out of Egypt even though the Pharaoh would be angry with him
- Keeping the Passover.

Yet God did not allow Moses to enter the Promised Land

because Moses had disobeyed him by striking a rock to bring water, instead of speaking to it, as God had instructed. God said Moses' actions showed he didn't believe God and didn't treat him as holy in the sight of the Israelites (see Nm 20:7-12). Yet in Hebrews 11 God commends him for his faithfulness. When Moses died, God summed up his ministry by saying: "Since then no prophet has risen in Israel like Moses, whom the Lord knew face to face, for all the signs and wonders which the Lord sent him to perform in the land of Egypt against Pharaoh, all his servants, and all his land, and for all the mighty power and for all the great terror which Moses performed in the sight of all Israel" (Dt 34:10-12, NASB). Moses didn't have a perfect record as a leader, and yet God praised him.

God is not like us, yet it's easy to project onto God our own attitudes and thoughts. If I haven't prayed for several days, I feel as if God is angry with me and might not listen to me because he's in a snit, saying, "Kathy who? She wants *my* attention? Who does she think she is? She only talks to me when she wants something from me. Forget that!"

But God never responds to us that way! He accepts, values, and appreciates the small efforts we make toward him. Any time we approach his presence, he welcomes us warmly and wholeheartedly. If we need forgiveness, he reaches out his arms and receives our confession. He always knows who we are and says to each one of us, "Come boldly, daughter, before my throne. You have my Son Jesus' robe of righteousness wrapped around you. You are perfect and beautiful in my eyes. I'm eager to listen and talk with you. I love you and care about what's important to you, even though you're not yet perfect."

God's approval and acceptance of us is *not* based on anything we do—except asking Jesus to be our Lord and Savior.

It's because of Jesus' death and resurrection that we are considered righteous in God's eyes. "The law was added so that the trespass might increase. But where sin increased, grace increased all the more, so that, just as sin reigned in death, so also grace might reign through righteousness to bring eternal life through Jesus Christ our Lord" (Rom 5:20-21). The perfectionist lives under the law, but God has given us grace.

Instead of aiming for 100 percent, we can understand that even 1 percent is valuable in God's eyes. I call this "the One Percent Principle." When we apply the One Percent Principle, we know that God is working in us, even if we don't see giant strides. We are able to give God praise for working in our lives.

If you struggle with "all or nothing" thinking, make it your goal to embrace the One Percent Principle.

Embrace the One Percent Principle

The following chart demonstrates the differences in thinking between a person who believes she must do things 100 percent and one who has embraced the One Percent Principle.

100 Percent Goal	One Percent Goal
I must never become angry with my children again.	I'm going to ask God to help me not to become angry today, especially between 5:00 and 6:00 P.M. And I'll ask Rhonda to pray for me during that time.

100 Percent Goal	One Percent Goal
I can't praise my toddler until he picks up all his toys.	I'm going to praise my toddler even when he picks up only five toys.
I'm never going to gossip again.	At the meeting on Tuesday evening, I'll pray for strength to refrain from gossiping, even if I have to say I don't want to hear someone's comments.
I can't give myself credit for finishing that project until it's completed.	I'm going to break that project into small goals and celebrate after each goal I attain.
I'll wait until I have an hour available to work on my Bible study.	I have seven minutes until I have to make that phone call; I'll anwer one question in my Bible study.
I've got to get everything completed on my to-do list in order to feel successful.	I'm going to trust God for my day and seek him for direction. Even if I only get one thing done and he directed it, then I can feel good about it.

Priscilla still lives in the left column, but she's learning to live in the right one. She says, "We bought a house a little over a year ago, and I have a huge to-do list. I get disappointed when my husband doesn't complete a chore, and that makes me angry. And then I have a hard time forgiving him for not completing it! ERRR!"

We perfectionists relate to Priscilla's struggle. But the truth is, praise encourages a person to be more motivated! Scripture tells us: "The wise in heart are called discerning, and pleasant words promote instruction. Understanding is a fountain of life to those who have it, but folly brings punishment to fools. A wise man's heart guides his mouth, and his lips promote instruction. Pleasant words are a honeycomb, sweet to the soul and healing to the bones" (Prv 16:21-24). If only we could get that into our brains!

Karissa told me, "I have to remember that my kids are no more perfect than I am. For young children, a half-done job is better than no job done at all. As a parent, I need to give more praise and fewer complaints."

Psychologist David A. Seamands confirms the need for small steps:

We must make clear there are no quick cures, no speedy solutions. Neither a miraculous Christian experience nor an instantaneous inner healing is likely to free one from the bonds of the performance trap, especially in its extreme perfectionistic forms. No one believes more than I do in the necessity of the new birth and life in the Spirit as *the* basic ingredients of the Christian life. However, I also believe that many Christians with damaged emotions and unhealed memories need a special kind of inner healing to enable them to live truly victorious lives. All this I find to be in complete agreement with biblical principles, but I consistently warn against solutions that are more magic than miracle, and sow confusion in the hearts of hurting Christians.[3]

Jeanette heard me share the One Percent Principle at a women's retreat. She worked full time and was exhausted by the end of the day. But her "all or nothing" thinking caused her to feel that she should cook the perfect meal at the perfect time. That meant every food group fixed in a fancy manner, within one hour of returning home, while helping her child with her homework. It not only drove her bonkers, she often gave up and ordered take-out food. In fact, she ordered dinner from the local Chinese take-out so often that the first time she actually showed up in person at that restaurant (instead of having the food delivered) and introduced herself as the woman from 23 Beech Street, the whole kitchen staff smiled and introduced themselves, and they gave her two free sodas!

After the retreat she wrote me that she had decided to apply the One Percent Principle. As a result, she started cooking simple meals that could be prepared easily. She even served things like scrambled eggs and toast, or pancakes and syrup once or twice a week. For dinner! Her daughter told her, "I am so proud of you, Mom. You are making dinner all the time now!"

By taking small steps and releasing "all or nothing" thinking, we'll find greater success in becoming who God wants us to be. Then we'll give God the credit and see his work in our lives.

Becky applied the One Percent Principle in another way. She told me: "I'm getting to a place where I am able to let go of my agenda. Recently, I've started my daily quiet times by visually giving my worries and burdens over to God for that day. Then I turn my focus to God's great attributes. I work hard at moving one step at a time. I consider the big work project I have and make a plan, breaking it down into many small steps. Then I focus on one step at a time. This way I can allow God to direct me through each step even when I'm overwhelmed."

Both Jeanette and Becky have found the key: allow God to work *little by little*.

I asked Barbara Johnson, popular Christian speaker and prolific author, to give me an illustration of the One Percent Principle. She applied it to giving praise and said:

> If someone came to me and said she was waiting to give praise to her husband until he did something 100 percent, I'd tell her, "You'll be waiting a long time." I don't feel that we should wait until something is done perfectly before we give praise. We can't expect perfection from others. I think that if your husband tries something, give him praise because he made an effort. Very few of them will do it the way we want, anyway. For instance, I'm thinking of the way my husband took out the trash today. He does it so laboriously, smashing down all the milk cartons, making everything as small as possible. He's a perfectionist and I'm not. He's so particular. Our trash is the smallest trash on the street because he wants it all folded down neatly. Instead of getting frustrated with him—because it doesn't work anyway—I enjoy our reputation in the neighborhood for having the smallest trash!

Like Barbara, we need to focus on the good (even if it's only 1 percent)! Does that mean we won't instruct our children on how to improve? Of course not. We will, but we must also focus on what they *did* accomplish, not just what they *didn't*.

One Percents Add Up!

When we learn to give ourselves credit for the small steps, God works in our lives—1 percent at a time! Those "one percents" eventually add up. My friend Mike Bechtle shared a story with me that exemplifies that.

Like most men, at the end of the day Mike pulled the coins out of his pockets and dropped them on the top of his dresser. As the coins accumulated, he put them in a shoebox in his closet because he hated to roll them.

One day his fourteen-year-old son, Tim, walked into his office and said, "Dad, can I roll those coins for you?"

Mike replied, "Tim, that'd be great. I'd really appreciate it."

Tim had an entrepreneurial spirit. "Can I keep 10 percent for my fee?"

Believing the shoebox contained about forty dollars, Mike figured it was worth four dollars to have him roll those coins.

After an hour or so, Tim came back to Mike and announced he was finished.

Mike replied, "That's great, Tim. Did you take your fee?"

"Sure did," Tim replied.

"How much did you get?" his dad asked.

"About thirty dollars," Tim announced.

Mike was aghast. "Tim, I told you to take only 10 percent."

"I did," Tim countered.

Quick math. Quick shock. "You mean I have three hundred dollars in that box?"

"Nope, now you have $270."

Mike's coins had added up faster than he thought. That's how it is with the small steps we take to combat our "all or nothing" thinking.

You Can Do It!

I returned from a speaking engagement late one evening and Larry met me in the hallway, grinning like a Cheshire cat. *What is he up to?* I wondered.

He said, "Come into the kitchen." I followed him there and with a flourish of his hand, he pointed to the dish-less sink. "I did the dishes for you!"

I was so pleased! I wrapped my arms around him for a hug, and as I looked over his shoulder, my eyes gazed upon pieces of food and puddles of milk curdling on the kitchen counter. *He didn't wipe off the counter!* I was amazed. *Anyone knows the dishes aren't finished until you do that.*

Just as I began to open my mouth to instruct him in proper dishwashing, I remembered the One Percent Principle and quickly changed what I was about to say. "Honey," I exclaimed, "I love it and you! Thanks so much for supporting me in this way!"

I was so glad I bit my tongue and appreciated his loving gift—even if it wasn't done perfectly. And, guess what? Larry did the dishes again the next evening! I bet he wouldn't have done them then—or the many times since then—if I'd criticized his efforts.

How will you give up an "all or nothing" attitude? How will you give praise or appreciation today or this week, even when the job isn't done perfectly? What 1 percent step will you take to correct perfectionist attitudes?

I know you can do it!

Five

~

I Should Have My Act Together by Now

A s we opened the door to the model home, I started comparing it to my own house. Walking through the living room, I exclaimed to Larry, "Oh, look at how everything is coordinated! The love seat and the drapes have the same fabric. Oh, I wish our house had something like that."

Larry just rolled his eyes.

Then we went into the master bath. "Oh, Honey, look at this. It's one of those Jacuzzi bathtubs, and it has lots of counter space around it for candles and knickknacks. Oh, this is what I really want someday."

As I continued to ooh and aah throughout the house, I felt my discontent rising. As we drove away an hour later, I mentally walked through that dream house again. *Oh, if only I could have a kitchen like that. And if we could landscape like that, wouldn't it be wonderful?* Even after we arrived home, I kept thinking about all the things our home didn't have that I have always wanted.

Later that afternoon my friend Janice called and raved about the kitchen gadget party I'd had the night before. "Oh, Kathy, that was fun, even if I bought too much. By the way, I just loved the pad you have on your window seat in the living room. I noticed it matches the fabric on your sofa. How did you get that made?"

I told her about the company where I'd taken the fabric and she said she'd contact them. After we hung up, I walked into the living room and looked it over with new eyes. I really did like the fabric on the sofa and window seat. The chairs looked nice with the coordinated fabric. *I guess it's not so bad after all!* I mused.

As I realized how I'd fallen back into my old habit of discontent, I mentally hit myself over the head. "Kathy," I rebuked myself, "you've been working on contentment for years. (You even wrote a book about it!) When are you ever going to learn it?"

I had fallen into one of the characteristics of the perfectionist—*again!* In the perfectionist's heart of hearts, something whispers, "I really thought I would be more mature by now! Look at how long I've worked at life!" Or, "I really thought I'd be more loving ... or content ... or self-controlled ... or ..." We believe that maturity means not struggling with the same things over and over again. We cry out, "Lord, I've already dealt with that situation. Do I have to face it again?"

We may have walked with the Lord a long time and learned much about the Bible and life. We think, *Shouldn't I be victorious over temptation? Shouldn't I have enough self-discipline to spend time in Bible reading and prayer every day? Shouldn't I be over my anger problem? Shouldn't I be able to resist the second piece of pie? Haven't I learned anything by now?*

Ironically, age has little to do with this kind of thinking. When I was fifteen I believed I was old enough to stop fighting with my sister. At age twenty-one I figured I shouldn't be angry with the customers at work because I'd been dealing with them for three years. When Darcy was born I considered myself an older mom and scolded myself for being nervous about caring for her. Regardless of our age, we think the experience we've gained should keep us from having to work on growing in an area over and over again. If our goal is perfection, it can seem like we aren't growing at all.

Several months after Larry and I visited that model home, my friend Lisa called to say she and her husband had purchased a new home. I was genuinely happy for her, and it wasn't until later that I realized how different this response had been from what I had felt previously. In the past I would have been jealous of such news, but God had been working on this weakness within me for a long time. It felt good to be free from thinking a new house would make me happy. I *had* grown!

But even as I rejoiced at how I'd changed, I toyed with the idea that, finally, I have my act together. But then I sensed the Lord very gently tapping my mental shoulder. "Daughter," he said compassionately within my heart, "you *have* done well in my power. Now I want you to work on your critical tongue."

As long as we are on this earth, we will always struggle with surrendering something to God. Instead of focusing on having a sinless life, we should focus on growing spiritually. We'll never be perfect, but we can learn, mature, and become more like Christ. Listen to these wise words from a recent letter I received:

I'm sixty-five and retired. My motto now? *Carpe diem.* I really want to do the Lord's will in whatever time I have left. Sometimes the so-called Golden Years aren't so golden. I had to work outside the home and raise a family, and didn't have much time to write, so I put it off. Now I am a part-time caretaker of a disabled husband, and my own health isn't all that wonderful. Life is just plain messy, I've decided—in addition to being what happens while you're planning other things!

Things don't get more perfect as we get older! We need to accept the "messiness" and see how God can use it for good.

We'll Encourage Others

Charles Swindoll writes, "Grace will help you let the cracks of your life show. Let them show! No one can identify with those who give the impression of nothing but flawless performances and slick success. We can all identify with failure and imperfection. And God has ways of honoring those times."[1]

He goes on to describe a time he preached a sermon with a sore throat and laryngitis. He could only whisper, which he found out later was the worst thing he could do, but he was determined to give his sermon. He writes:

I felt my delivery was terrible. I thought it was the worst job I had ever done. Then something surprising happened. I don't know how many people contacted me later and said, "You'll never know how that ministered to me." There I was in obvious physical weakness and pain ... hindered, restrained by something I could not control or stop. Yet it became encouragement to others, especially those who said they wondered if I ever struggled with weaknesses. Immediately, they could identify with me rather than view me from a distance in some sort of unrealistic admiration.[2]

As I read those words, I was reminded of what Paul wrote in 2 Corinthians 12:8-10:

Three times I pleaded with the Lord to take it away from me. But he said to me, "My grace is sufficient for you, for my power is made perfect in weakness." Therefore I will boast all the more gladly about my weaknesses, so that Christ's power may rest on me. That is why, for Christ's sake, I delight in weaknesses, in insults, in hardships, in persecutions, in difficulties. For when I am weak, then I am strong.

According to this text, God's power can be made manifest through our weaknesses (not our strengths)! I believe that's what happened to Pastor Swindoll, and it's also what can happen for you and me when we ask God to use us despite our weaknesses and struggles.

When I was physically abusing my daughter, I believed that if I told my friends about my struggle I would lose all credibility with them. I even feared that some might doubt God's faithfulness. But once I had the courage to confess my behavior and ask for prayer, they became involved in my healing. They began praying for me and holding me accountable. Each week at Bible study they would ask me, "How was your anger this past week, Kathy?" As I shared my progress, they saw God delivering me. Their trust in God increased as they saw God's powerful hand at work in my life. They knew God could help them in the situations they faced.

We'll Become More Like Christ

When you and I continue to be "in process" spiritually, we grow into the image of Jesus Christ. Growth often comes through adversity. Growth in our character happens only when we have experiences that stretch us. As we grow, we'll be more:

Humble: If you and I were suddenly healed or delivered from every weakness or difficulty—and became perfect—we might become proud and think, "Why can't everyone get healed or delivered like me? They must not have the faith I do." Our struggle against sin keeps us humble.

Dependent on God: If we didn't need to look to God for strength in our fight against sin, we might think, *I don't really need your help anymore, Lord. I can handle the rest by myself, thanks very much.* Such an attitude fails to remember that we need to rely upon God's power moment by moment, whether or not we're facing a major difficulty.

In Philippians 1:6 Paul says: "Being confident of this, that he who began a good work in you will carry it on to completion until the day of Christ Jesus." The *New American Standard Bible* phrases this verse this way: "For I am confident of this very thing, that He who began a good work in you will *perfect* it until the day of Christ Jesus" (emphasis mine). God is committed to molding and shaping us into the image of Christ. Every trial, struggle, difficulty, and relationship that we face is God's handiwork to make us depend on him and correct any wrong ideas we have about him.

Isaiah 25:1 comforts us with the good news that God plans everything for our lives. "O Lord, you are my God; I will exalt you and praise your name, for in perfect faithfulness you have done marvelous things, things planned long ago." Although he doesn't create the bad things, he allows them so we can get to know him more.

Sensitive to others' pain: If our lives were trouble-free, we might avoid meeting the needs of others. It's easy to tell ourselves, "If I'm not in pain, I don't think anyone else should be either. They need to get a life." But suffering can give us different eyes.

My friend Lois has experienced this. Her husband Dan died over a year ago. She recently told me that before he died, she felt she was prepared for his death. She and Dan had talked openly with their family and friends about what they were going through, and they cried easily and often. Lois said that she had wondered if she would suffer any grief at all after Dan died because they had grieved together.

But that's not what happened. Lois' grief has been intense. She still cries at anything that reminds her of Dan—and as she puts it, "that's everything I see or experience." She sometimes berates herself for her tears; she's tempted to think that she should be completely healed *by now.*

She went on to tell me that she is beginning to see God's purpose in her grief. She's become more compassionate. Before Dan's death she would get impatient if someone didn't heal as quickly in an area as she might have. The intensity of Lois' pain has also made her more humble and dependent on God. In the past she looked to Dan to take care of things. Now she's making decisions she never wrestled with before. This has deepened her awareness of her need for God's guidance. And God has caused her to be even more passionate about her relationship with him. She thought she was close to him, but she says, "I didn't have a clue as to how close I could become. Now I can't divert any attention onto Dan. God is my all in all and we have a running conversation every moment."

We'll Experience God's Patience

God isn't in a hurry like we are. He is working within us little by little. He's not impatiently tapping his toe waiting for us to become perfect. It's OK with him that you and I are "in process."

The apostle Paul told Timothy: "Do not neglect your gift, which was given you through a prophetic message when the body of elders laid their hands on you. Be diligent in these matters; give yourself wholly to them, so that everyone may see your progress" (1 Tm 4:14-15). Although Paul was referring to spiritual gifts in this verse, it contains a basic principle that perfectionists desperately need to hear: *spiritual growth is a process.*

When I first studied this verse, I was surprised Paul used the word "progress." I would have stressed *perfection*, not progress! Progress is so ... imperfect! (Aren't you glad God didn't want *me* to write that verse?)

W.E. Vine identifies *progress* as the Greek word *prokopē*, meaning *pro* (forward) and *kopiō* (to cut). He wrote, "Originally the word was used of a pioneer cutting his way through brushwood."[3] As I read that explanation, I felt like yelling, "Eureka!" Those words contained the perfect description of the way God wants us to view our earthly process of growth—and his patience. (At least some things in life are perfect!)

But the perfectionist sees it differently. A pioneer who was a perfectionist would have gone out onto her land, surveyed the job, and pulled out a mile-long scythe. With one *SWOOSH!* she would cut a wide swath. Her house would be built by noon! Don't laugh! Isn't that the way we want it to happen?

Yet that's not how it works. Over and over, little by little, we cut our way through the brushwood until there's space to begin building our house, board by board. It's all a process! God is patiently working in our lives little by little, step by step, 1 percent at a time.

God doesn't expect us to be perfect, just growing! We don't have to arrive; we just have to keep on the journey. Kendra made that discovery. In a recent Email she wrote:

> I recently thought over the big and little things that have happened in the last two years and how God has helped me control my once-consuming anger. In fact, two weeks ago, I remember standing at my sink washing dishes, with the kids fighting in the background and macaroni and cheese (again!) bubbling on the stove, when a thought hit me out of nowhere. I AM HAPPY! I am happy being a mother. It had seemed so long since I felt that joy, and it is so good to have it back. It's partly because the kids are getting older and easier to care for (and someday maybe we'll be done with DIAPERS!!!!). But the real reason is the work God is patiently performing in my life daily. He is so good. I know I have a long way to go, but considering that last Christmas I was thinking about suicide or running away, I praise God for giving me a miracle. I now rely on Christ and his Word in such a deep way. But the amazing thing is that it was a

step-by-step process, and some days those were pretty tiny steps, but they all add up.

Like Kendra, we don't have to be discouraged that we aren't maturing fast enough. God is responsible for the timing. He patiently leads us through each step of the process. We can paint a portrait in our minds of God with outstretched hands, his voice soothingly telling us, "Daughter, it's OK. I'm not in a hurry. I know the plans I have for you and it's for your benefit and growth. You'll be going through this until the moment you see me face to face!" That's what God imparted in Jeremiah 29:11: "'For I know the plans I have for you,' declares the Lord, 'plans to prosper you and not to harm you, plans to give you hope and a future.'"

How Can I Cooperate With God in the Process?

We all smile at the thought of a little girl who considers herself too short, standing on her tiptoes, trying to stretch her body. That little girl *will* grow, but she can't force it to happen. She just needs to eat good food, run on the school playground, and have fun for all she's worth. In the same way, we can't force spiritual growth to happen, but we can cooperate with God's work within us through surrendering to God's power. Let's consider how to do that.

Get help from others. When we are weak, whether physically, emotionally, or spiritually, we often feel ashamed and hide our feelings. We can become discouraged rather than rejoicing in how God's power can walk us through the problems of life.

Often God uses others to encourage and strengthen us, while at the same time using us to encourage others.

As a perfectionist you might have trouble reaching out for help, even though that's the very time you need others the most. The author of Hebrews wrote, "And let us consider how we may spur one another on toward love and good deeds. Let us not give up meeting together, as some are in the habit of doing, but let us encourage one another—and all the more as you see the Day approaching" (10:24-25).

For example, if you're struggling with gossip, confess it and ask for prayer support. You may inspire someone else to acknowledge her same tendency.

If you're feeling depressed, don't keep it a secret. Call a good friend and say, "I need to do something fun. Can we go window shopping?"

If you're feeling confused about a decision you must make, don't give the impression you have all the wisdom in the world. Seek the counsel of a prudent friend. When you do, you'll find that instead of disappointing others with your imperfections, you'll actually encourage them *and* receive the strength you need.

Not every friend will be the best person to tell. Some women can't be honest enough to see their own struggles and therefore can't receive anyone else's. Others truly don't believe Christians should struggle. If your friend is a "just fix it" person, she may not allow you to be in a process of growth.

Pray and ask the Lord to direct you to someone who can help. As you do, take into account:

- How has this person responded to you in the past when you've been honest?
- Has she helped others who are struggling?

- What kind of personality is she?
- Has she struggled very much herself? It seems that women who have their own struggles are more helpful with practical ideas.
- Does she seem to keep the confidences of others or does she gossip?
- How available is she to spend time with you, to walk you through this time of difficulty?

You may not be able to find someone who fits all these criteria. But the more she does, the more helpful her response will be.

Make a choice to accept—even rejoice in—those imperfections that make you dependent on God. No one loves the process of change and growth. No one says, "Bring it on, Lord!" But we can say, "OK, Lord, I'm always going to be in process, and since it'll bring me closer to you, I choose to accept it. I'll even choose to be joyful about the good that will come from this struggle. Help me to see you in each trial I face."

Author Barbara Johnson told me, "The time comes when you realize there's never a time when we can say we have it all together. As long as we accept that, realizing there's always something new around the corner, life seems much easier. Things will go much better if we accept everyone's imperfections. This is a broken world we're living in. Everything's broken. Once we accept that, you don't expect perfection from everything you run into."

Barbara is right. The next time you disappoint yourself, make a choice to accept your imperfection and say out loud, "This is a broken world, and I can't expect myself to be perfect." The next time your neighbor forgets to take in the garbage can, say out loud, "This is a broken world, and I can't expect them to be perfect." The next time your pastor doesn't return your call and you feel neglected, say out loud, "This is a broken world, and I can't expect even him to be perfect." Let the truth of this world's limitations seep deeply into your heart, and give up expecting perfection from yourself or others. And choose to rejoice in the good things that result from the progress you're making.

Ask God to show you how he's using you in spite of your imperfections. Melanie gave me an example of how God uses imperfect people. She was at a weekend retreat with two friends, one who was the key speaker and another who was praying for the individual needs of the women at the retreat. As Melanie watched these two women ministering to others, God whispered to her, "Melanie, I've used you in their spiritual growth." Melanie wanted to weep, because in her mind she had so often failed those women. How could God have used her in their lives?

During the weekend, Melanie and her two friends went for a long walk together. She tried to tell them what God was showing her, but she felt embarrassed. Finally she blurted out, "I don't want to sound proud, but God told me he has used me to help you both grow into the sensitive prayer ministers and leaders that you are."

One of Melanie's friends reached over and hugged her. "Mel, you're right. It's been your neediness and desperation for God that has taught me to pray and seek God. Don't you see? God is so much larger than your mistakes."

As Melanie discovered, if we rejoice in how God uses us in spite of our imperfections, maybe our journey through the brushwood won't seem so daunting and endless. We discover there's purpose in it!

I think that's what Max Lucado was writing about in his book *On the Anvil.* He wrote:

On God's anvil. Perhaps you've been there.

Melted down. Formless. Undone. Placed on the anvil ... for reshaping? (A few rough edges too many.) Discipline? ("A good father disciplines.") Testing? (But why so hard?)

I know. I've been on it. It's rough. It's a spiritual slump, a famine. The fire goes out. Although the fire may flame for a moment, it soon disappears. We drift downward. Downward into the foggy valley of question, the misty lowland of discouragement. Motivation wanes. Desire is distant. Responsibilities are depressing.

Passion? It slips out the door.

Enthusiasm? Are you kidding?

Anvil time.

It can be caused by a death, a breakup, going broke, going prayerless. The light switch is flipped off and the room darkens. "All the thoughtful words of help and hope have all been nicely said. But I'm still hurting, wondering...."

On the anvil.

Brought face-to-face with God out of the utter realization that we have nowhere else to go. Jesus in the garden. Peter with a tear-streaked face. David after Bathsheba. Elijah and the "still, small voice." Paul, blind in Damascus.

Pound, pound, pound.

I hope you're not on the anvil. (Unless you need to be, and if so, I hope you are.) Anvil time is not to be avoided; it's to be experienced. Although the tunnel is dark, it does go through the mountain. Anvil time reminds us of who we are and who God is. We shouldn't try to escape it. To escape it could be to escape God.

God sees our life from beginning to end. He may lead us through a storm at age thirty so we can endure a hurricane at age sixty. An instrument is useful only if it's in the right shape. A dull ax or a bent screwdriver needs attention, and so do we. A good blacksmith keeps his tools in shape. So does God.

Should God place you on his anvil, be thankful. It means he thinks you're still worth reshaping.[4]

If we think we should have arrived, we're trying to jump off the anvil. Of course, God *will* make progress in our lives, but did you think that meant you'd have perfect patience? Did you think your relationships would all go smoothly? Did you think inappropriate comments wouldn't ever spill out of your mouth? Did you think you'd never have times of discontent?

Yes, I'm speaking to myself as I write, that it's all right that we haven't arrived yet. God is still working on us. Yes, there's still much brushwood ahead, but God is guiding our scythe with every *SWOOSH!* He's not impatient. Neither should we be. He knows exactly the plan that he has for us, for our growth and progress. Just keep raising and lowering the scythe.

Six

My Expectations Tend to Be Unrealistic

Several months ago, I planned to join Larry in San Diego after he completed the first day of a conference he was attending. As I drove south, I envisioned a romantic dinner at a nice restaurant, with some great cuddling in his hotel room afterward.

I arrived at the hotel, and Larry met me at the desk with a tight hug and kiss. Great start! Then he introduced me to some of his friends, and we visited for a few moments. We excused ourselves, put my luggage in his room, then walked to the car. Larry said, "I've been eating so much food today, Kathy, I really need to eat small tonight. I was thinking we could go to McDonald's for dinner. It's their Wednesday sale of twenty-nine-cent hamburgers! We can just go through the drive-through and eat in the room as we watch the news."

McDonald's? Hamburgers? News? I'd expected dinner in a romantic setting with great food and a luscious dessert. Not exactly fast food! Nor drive-through! Thoughts swirled through my brain: *Larry should know how important a romantic dinner is to me. Since he's not making it a priority, he must not really love me. I'll pout in order to communicate my displeasure. If he doesn't inquire about my silence and then change his mind, then*

85

I'll know he doesn't care about me.

Even after twenty-nine years of marriage and years of trying to overcome my perfectionist tendencies, the old patterns of thinking still bubbled up—but only initially. As soon as those thoughts popped into my mind, I knew I could make a choice to resist those old patterns. Thankfully, I've learned that those old responses don't bring the results I want and need. In that moment, I was able to say, "Well, Honey, that *is* disappointing because I'd really hoped we could have a romantic dinner. Are you sure?"

Larry knew from my words and the tone of my voice that I was disappointed, and he replied, "I'm sorry, but we had a huge lunch and snacks available all day. I'm filled to the gills. Can we delay a romantic dinner until tomorrow night? And I'll drive through any place you want tonight."

At that point, I had another choice. Would I mentally rehearse the times Larry had disappointed me, or would I focus on the times he had shown me his love? Would I fall back into my old perfectionist patterns of expecting Larry to perform *perfectly* in order for me to feel loved, or could I be selfless and understand his need for a small portion of food?

It wasn't easy because I don't prefer being noble or selfless, but I said, "Honey, I understand. I'll take McDonald's tonight if we can go big tomorrow. OK?"

"OK."

I wish I could say my disappointment didn't nag me all evening, but I can't. It was something I battled as we ate our hamburgers, watched the news, and then cuddled. But at least I made the 1 percent improvement of recognizing quickly that I'd set up expectations that were *my* idea of perfection—*not* Larry's.

Great Expectations

We perfectionists often have unrealistic expectations. Even though we may say we know a perfect life is unattainable, we tell ourselves that our expectations are realistic, attainable, and in line with the way everyone else thinks. If those expectations aren't met or considered important by others, we feel hurt and find it hard to release our predetermined hopes. And if someone has truly wounded us, intentionally or not, we have a hard time forgiving them.

Our expectations can go from the ordinary to the extreme. Sally expected her husband to throw a surprise fiftieth birthday party for her. Doreen thought her roommate should always clean up her dishes immediately after finishing a meal. Krista longed for her boyfriend to bring a corsage for her on their dates. Sondra believed her husband should plan a getaway weekend for their anniversary. Deidre expected her children to behave perfectly in public.

We can easily develop these expectations and then add mental baggage to them. The baggage includes ideas like:

- I shouldn't have to tell him or her what I want; he or she should read my mind.
- This is something normal that everyone else wants or does.
- If it's important to me, it should be just as important to them.

Such ideas are based on the incorrect assumption that everyone thinks (or should think) the same way we do!

Am I saying that all expectations are wrong? Absolutely not! Expectations are normal. Everyone has them. But when we insist that our expectations be met, we get into trouble.

Evaluate Our Expectations

How, then, can we let go of or adjust unrealistic expectations? When we find ourselves feeling angry, disappointed, or hurt by someone, it's important to understand why. Often such feelings are due to our expectations. The first action we can take is to identify our expectations. What were we expecting to happen? Is this realistic or unrealistic? Once we have identified our expectation, we need to evaluate it.

Here are some guidelines that can help you as you evaluate your expectations. Ask yourself:

Does this person know what I expect or want? Sometimes our expectations aren't met simply because the person doesn't know what we are thinking! When we tell others what we want, we give them the opportunity to fulfill our desires.

I was reminded of this recently when our family dined at an expensive restaurant. Even though I felt the salad was inferior, I didn't say anything—I didn't want to "make a scene" by complaining. But as I thought about it later, I realized I could have asked for a different salad in a *pleasant* way. Such a request wasn't inappropriate and wouldn't have spoiled our evening.

The next week while out to lunch, my steak was undercooked. Rather than suffering in silence, I expressed my dissatisfaction to the waitress. She said, "No problem," and sent the steak back to the kitchen to be properly cooked. I left the restaurant feeling happy and satisfied.

We can express our expectations in a healthy way, without waiting for our anger to propel us into a tirade. We can avoid becoming disappointed in imperfect circumstances because we believed someone should automatically know what we wanted.

What does the Bible have to say about this expectation? The most important question we can ask is whether or not our idea agrees with what God has to say about the subject. If our idea doesn't match his Word, we don't have to go any farther. We can eliminate that expectation.

Early in our marriage I thought I could change Larry by pouting and complaining when he wouldn't do something I wanted him to do. When my attempts to manipulate him didn't work, I got very angry. In time I began to see that God wanted me to work on my response—not on changing my husband! Philippians 2:14 told me, "Do everything without complaining or arguing." Proverbs 21:19 instructed me, "Better to live in a desert than with a quarrelsome and ill-tempered wife."

It has taken years, but I've gotten much better about telling Larry what I want without any demands that he meet my desires. I'm learning to turn over my expectations to God and allow him to change Larry.

If we expect something that God hasn't promised or that disagrees with God's Word, then we're counting on something that's not going to happen. We must consistently study the Bible to find out God's viewpoint, and then follow it.

Ask for other people's input. I can still remember the day I had an unrealistic expectation corrected through the input of my neighbor, Candy. As a child I'd been trained to wash sheets every week, and I'd continued that habit into my married life. With two toddlers, life was hectic, but I felt guilty if I didn't wash the sheets every week.

Then one day Candy and I were talking and the topic of washing sheets came up. Candy surprised me when she said, "Oh, I wash our sheets every two or three weeks."

Every two or three weeks? I couldn't believe it. I wanted to say, "You mean it's OK to do that?" Somehow I had believed that anyone who was a good housekeeper washed her sheets each week. I felt as if the world would cave in if I waited any longer.

But after my conversation with Candy, I relaxed and washed the sheets less often. As a result, I had less stress in my life. Getting Candy's input helped me to adjust my unrealistic expectations.

The next time you're evaluating whether one of your expectations is realistic, get the input of others. That's the benefit of getting together with others, especially Christians, who can share their perspective of God and his Word.

Why is this so important to me? Most of the time, our unrealistic expectations are founded upon wanting to build up our own sense of worth. This question can help reveal our true motives.

For instance, if you expect your husband to bring you some flowers, ask yourself whether it's because you long to know you're securely loved and you think this would prove that you are. Or if you think a friend should send you a get well card when you're sick, ask if it's because you want to know your friendship is important to her. Most of us are looking for reassurances that we are loved and important. Therefore, we form expectations that will support our need for affirmation.

But not everyone thinks the same way we do (although it's human to assume otherwise!). Just because *you* send a card to indicate a friendship is important, your friend may not. Whether she sends you a get well card probably has nothing to do with the importance she places on your friendship. I frequently receive Email postcards and greeting cards from friends, but rarely think to initiate them myself. Are my friends important to me? Of course. Do I love and value them? Of course. But if they are expecting me to affirm that love and value through Email cards, their expectations may not be met.

If you struggle in this area, ask God to help you go to him for affirmation of your worth and value. People—even those who care deeply about us—will always disappoint us. Only God never fails.

Where did this idea come from? Many times we are influenced subtly by people and circumstances without knowing it. By looking for the source of our expectations, we may be more adept at adjusting them and making them realistic.

About the time Pamela and her husband, Craig, celebrated their first anniversary, Pamela's father went through a midlife crisis and left Pamela's mother (although they eventually reconciled). Because her parents fought frequently throughout their marriage, Pamela unconsciously began to believe she and Craig shouldn't fight or else he would leave her—like her dad had left her mom.

As soon as Craig would become intense or loud about an issue, Pamela would panic, run out of the house, and drive off in the car. In her mind, if you disagreed with each other you didn't love each other. She just couldn't handle the idea of an argument. She wanted to have a marriage that was perfect and problem-free.

In time, Pamela realized that her expectation of never disagreeing or arguing was unrealistic. She and Craig could work out their disagreements through discussion. Sometimes they might even raise their voices. This didn't mean they didn't love each other, only that they cared enough not to sweep problems under the rug.

Hold Expectations Loosely and Choose to Forgive

Not only do we need to learn to identify, understand, and express our expectations, we also have to learn to hold them—even realistic expectations—loosely and to forgive those who hurt or disappoint us. Sometimes people are not able (or are unwilling) to meet our expectations, even if those expectations are reasonable and communicated. Only God is capable of meeting our needs fully. Only he knows exactly what we truly need. In fact, he knows better than we do what our needs are, and he promises to meet those needs. "And my God will meet all your needs according to his glorious riches in Christ Jesus" (Phil 4:19).

Author and popular Christian speaker Lee Ezell had to come to grips with the fact that her father did not love and nurture her. She was faced with a choice of whether to forgive him and let go of her expectation that he love her, or to hang on to her hurt and become bitter and resentful. She writes:

After he died, in my quest to develop loving feelings for him, I began to look for redeeming factors and some explanation of his intolerable behavior. I was thirty-five years old before I got the answers I needed, stumbling across some background information that was enlightening and helpful. I was never told that my father was abandoned as a child, raised by reluctant relatives who changed his name, resulting in a haunting feeling of rejection. At this point of discovery I realized I had a choice. I could either keep my justified resentment toward my dad and dismiss the new information as "no excuse for putting his children through hell," or I could factor it into the picture. Because I knew it was God's will that I choose to love, I picked the higher path. In making this effort, love and understanding for my deceased dad began to grow. I found myself regretting that I hadn't known more about him while he was still alive. It might have made a difference.

Today when I think of my father as *Daddy*, I don't get the old stabbing pain of resentment. I am less aware of the pain of abandonment and loss. Instead, I feel a sense of warmth, realizing that he was a broken man, emotionally deformed and crippled by life's injustices, who was merely doing the best he could.[1]

Lee understands that in this imperfect world, even appropriate expectations don't always get met. Because of this, we must hold them loosely, trusting God to give us what we need. God, our perfect Daddy, says, "Daughter, only I can meet your needs perfectly. Seek me. Base your expectations upon what I can provide and hold loosely the expectations of what others can give. They will fail but I will not, because I love you perfectly."

Lee chose to forgive her father for failing to love her. This is key to healing a wounded heart.

What Is Forgiveness?

When a person fails to keep her promise or betrays our trust, the hurt can go deep. It's human to want to make that person suffer for the way she hurt us, but ultimate healing comes through forgiveness. Though we may understand the importance of forgiveness and our part in forgiving others, it may be helpful to consider what forgiving does not mean.

Forgiving doesn't mean there shouldn't be justice or consequences. Even if we can't administer justice, we have a just and righteous God who will punish the unrighteous for their evil deeds. Our righteous Judge says, "My eyes are on all their ways; they are not hidden from me, nor is their sin concealed from my eyes. I will repay them double for their wickedness and their sin, because they have defiled my land with the lifeless forms of their vile images and have filled my inheritance with their detestable idols" (Jer 16:17-18). As a result, you and I can forgive because God will ensure there are consequences.

Forgiving doesn't mean I must allow someone to continue to mistreat me. Such thinking confuses forgiveness and trust. They are not the same. Author Dr. Chuck Lynch clarifies that when he writes, "Forgiveness and trust are two separate issues.... Forgiveness must be granted; trust has to be earned."[2]

I've talked to wives of husbands who have been unfaithful. Often they are confused about how to respond when their husband repents. They want to know: Should I move back in with him? Should we be intimate? Should I require that he stay away from the woman he sinned with?

Of course, every situation and person is unique, but typically it's not wise to trust automatically in this kind of situation. Trust comes with the assurance that an unfaithful spouse is making the appropriate changes and will no longer mistreat you.

Likewise an adult daughter who forgives her mother for constantly criticizing her shouldn't feel obligated to visit her mother, unless the mother makes changes in the way she treats her daughter. A mother whose child has been sexually abused by her stepfather doesn't have to leave the daughter in his care even though he has "confessed and repented." A woman doesn't have to subject herself to her friend's constant gossip about their acquaintances, even if she forgives her. God wants us to protect ourselves—even if we've forgiven that person.

Forgiving doesn't mean forgetting. Although God can forget when he forgives, he did not make humans able to do that. Pattie told me, "I guess I really haven't forgiven Julie for breaking her promise to help me with the decorations at the retreat. I thought I had, but I still feel angry toward her sometimes. When will I forgive her? I want to!"

I assured Pattie she had indeed forgiven Julie, but that forgiveness is not only a one-time choice; it's also a process. It's something we must do over and over again. We begin by making a decision with our wills, but the hurt feelings may remain. That doesn't mean we haven't forgiven; it means we'll have to affirm our decision over and over again when the negative feelings surface.

Because perfectionists have an "all or nothing" attitude, we might think that once we have forgiven, the pain should never resurface. But that's simply not true. It will still take time for the wound to heal even though we've taken the first step toward forgiveness.

As we eliminate these wrong perceptions about forgiveness, we'll be able to more freely forgive—something Jesus commanded us to do. He didn't qualify it by saying, "if they ask for your forgiveness," or, "after they are truly sorry." He commands us to forgive "seventy-seven times" (Mt 18:21-22), a reference to completeness or thoroughness. And because it's a command, it's not based on our feelings. It's a choice—something we do with our wills.

How Do I Forgive?

Although we aren't guaranteed good feelings, we can trust God to supply whatever we truly need in order to forgive someone. If you want to forgive, don't wait until you feel like it. Follow these guidelines:

Just do it! Even though it's not easy, we can do it. But there are times when I have to pray, "Lord, I can't forgive that person. But I'm willing to be made willing to do it."

Tammy had to make that choice after her husband, Ryan, disappointed her when she discovered he was addicted to phone sex. She was angry and revengeful. Her expectation of a perfect marriage was so shattered she couldn't even sleep in the same bed with him, even though Ryan had confessed, had turned away from his sin, and was in counseling with her. Her pain was just too great.

She vowed, "I will make Ryan pay. Not only will I be mean to him every day, I will never make lasagna for him again. Never! That will teach him! He can just suffer without his favorite food for the rest of his life." She also unconsciously punished him by gaining fifty-two pounds and becoming critical of everything he did.

Then, three months later, she talked with her sister, who talked excitedly about her pastor's sermon on 2 Corinthians 2:5-11. Several days later, Tammy was praying—something she'd begun doing more of—and reading her Bible. She turned to the passage her sister had raved about and was amazed at what she read:

If anyone has caused grief, he has not so much grieved me as he has grieved all of you, to some extent—not to put it too severely. The punishment inflicted on him by the majority is sufficient for him. Now instead, you ought to forgive and comfort him, so that he will not be overwhelmed by excessive sorrow. I urge you, therefore, to reaffirm your love for him. The reason I wrote you was to see if you would stand the test and be obedient in everything. If you forgive anyone, I also forgive him. And what I have forgiven—if there was anything to forgive—I have forgiven in the sight of Christ for your sake, in order that Satan might not outwit us. For we are not unaware of his schemes.

2 CORINTHIANS 2:5-11

Tammy felt as if God had jabbed her heart, and she wasn't happy about it! "That's not fair," she complained. "God, I shouldn't have to do anything. He's the one who messed up—not me!"

But Tammy knew what God was telling her: forgive Ryan or Satan would take advantage of her. "I didn't want Satan to have control over me. As I surrendered in that moment, God's peace that passes all understanding filled me because I suddenly had a plan! It was a God-inspired, life-breathed plan! But could I do it?" She knew the Lord was telling her to make lasagna for Ryan.

Tammy replied, "OK, Lord, I'll try!"

Even though she struggled to obey, Tammy took her children to a friend's house and prepared the special meal. "There were more tears than cheese in that lasagna as I let God soften my heart and mold me." When Ryan arrived home, Tammy expressed her love for him and promised to forgive him, even if it took time. He was so overwhelmed that he cried and apologized even more thoroughly than he'd done before. "I was amazed at his gentleness. My love for him started to rekindle."

Now, several years later, Tammy and Ryan's love for each other has blossomed into a beautiful love affair. Tammy says, "I often encounter people who ask about my favorite food, and I want to shout from the depths of my heart—lasagna!"

Are you willing to be made willing to forgive that person who has disappointed you and broken a promise to meet your expectations? Just do it! Take that first step.

Look for the positives. Elisabeth Elliot gives us wise advice when she writes:

> Many women have told me that my husband's advice, which I once quoted in a book, has been an eye-opener to them. He said that a wife, if she is very generous, may allow that her husband lives up to perhaps eighty percent of her expectations. There is always the other twenty percent that she would like to change, and she may chip away at it for the whole of their married life without reducing it by very much. She may, on the other hand, simply decide to enjoy the eighty percent, and both of them will be happy. It's a down-to-earth illustration of a principle: *Accept, positively and actively, what is given.* Let thanksgiving be the habit of your life.
>
> Such acceptance is not possible without a deep and abiding belief in the sovereign love of God. Either he is in charge, or he is not. Either he loves us, or he does not. If he is in charge and loves us, then whatever is given is subject to his control and is meant ultimately for our joy.[3]

Our *perspective* will determine whether we respond in a godly manner when our expectations are unfulfilled. Are you going to keep waiting for life to become perfect and be constantly resentful? Or are you going to focus on what is fulfilling and be grateful? Each of us makes that choice moment by moment. What will you do?

Trust God. Do you believe that God is sovereign? Sovereignty means that God is ultimately in complete control of our lives, reigning over everything that happens on earth. It was that kind of faith that enabled Joseph—whose story is told in the Book of Genesis—to be able to forgive his brothers after they taunted him for his dreams, hated him as the favored son of their father, and then sold him into slavery. "Joseph said to them, 'Don't be afraid. Am I in the place of God? You intended to harm me, but God intended it for good to accomplish what is now being done, the saving of many lives. So then, don't be afraid. I will provide for you and your children.' And he reassured them and spoke kindly to them" (50:20-21).

If God has allowed your expectations to go unmet, then he has a better plan. If someone has deeply hurt you, know that God wants you to forgive that person so that your character will be developed.

Are your needs unmet? Have you expressed them appropriately, or are you expecting that person to read your mind? Instead of letting your attitude slip into bitterness or resentment, express yourself in a godly manner and give the person the opportunity to meet your needs. Yet, hold your expectations loosely. That person may not be able—or willing—to meet them. Then you must look exclusively to your heavenly Father, who desires to meet all your *true* needs. This earth will never satisfy, and the people around us will invariably disappoint us. But as we forgive, we will show the world around us the true nature of us who have been forgiven so much.

Seven

"Good" Is Rarely "Good Enough"

Carolyn claims she was the "original" perfectionist. Nothing was ever "good enough." She couldn't stop at just dusting the furniture, she had to polish it to a high shine. If there was a spot in the corner of the kitchen floor, she cleaned the whole floor. She vacuumed every day and wouldn't allow her young children to walk on the carpet because it would mess up the nap. After someone used the bathroom sink, Carolyn rushed in to wipe down the counter, mirror, and wood cabinet. Her husband, Ted, often said jokingly that if he got up in the middle of the night to go to the bathroom, Carolyn would have the bed made by the time he got back.

But Carolyn's compulsions were no laughing matter. Her viewpoint that nothing was ever good enough brought chaos into her family, marriage, and home. She was frequently angry at the children for making messes, and she badgered her husband about picking up his clothes and not leaving clutter. Even if he tried to please her, she could always find some small way he could have done it better.

One time, wanting to surprise Carolyn when she was returning from a church retreat, and knowing she'd be tired, Ted prepared dinner for her. But when he set the garlic bread on the table, Carolyn commented that he should have broiled it farther from the flame so that the edges wouldn't be burned. And when the casserole was a little runny, she frowned and ate only one bite. She didn't even thank Ted for his effort.

On another occasion she was in the doctor's office, and the doctor dropped a piece of paper on the floor. She picked it up and heard her doctor say, "I knew you were that kind of a person who would *have* to pick it up!" This was followed, of course, by a lecture about "letting go of the small stuff." But Carolyn didn't listen. It just didn't make any sense to her. To her, *everything* was big stuff! And whether big or little, when it came to cleanliness, preparation, or attractiveness, the *ultimate* was always the goal.

Those outside her family circle thought Carolyn was the calmest woman in the world. No one suspected the private turmoil going on inside of her. But she was miserable, and the emotional stress was taking a physical toll on her. One day Carolyn finally decided, "Enough! No more! This is not living, it is merely existing." At her invitation, God began to work in a miraculous way. She told me, "God directed me to a woman who took one look at me and exclaimed, 'What happened to you?' She saw what was happening on the inside of me."

As Carolyn and her new friend spent many hours together, her friend encouraged her to rededicate her life to God. She says, "In time the Lord penetrated the wall of my perfectionism and literally crushed it. I began to see the devastating effects it was having on me and my family."

Today, Carolyn rejoices in God's great goodness, saying, "His mercies are new every day. I now have no problem letting go of the small stuff. My house is clean enough to be healthy and dirty enough to be happy."

Carolyn had to experience a tremendous healing to arrive

where she is today. And one of the things she learned is the difference between perfectionism and excellence. Excellence allows her to live with a little dirt!

Excellence Versus Perfectionism

I've found that most people make no distinction between excellence and perfection. To many, they are one and the same: the ultimate attainment of doing something completely and perfectly. But there is a clear difference: perfection is doing something perfectly, and excellence is doing the best you can, though the result is imperfect.

> Perfectionists often mistakenly label their compulsive, "I've got to do it right" behavior as a "quest for excellence." In truth, excellence and perfectionism are poles apart. The seeker of excellence tries to do her best and is satisfied with a solid, honest effort. The perfectionist seeks to be the best and is continually frustrated and defeated because she knows she "could have done it even better if..."[1]

The person who strives for perfection is never satisfied with the level of progress, cleanliness, performance, or effort she's made. She can't concentrate on what she's done well because she's focused on what she could have done.

In contrast, the person who strives for excellence is satisfied with her best effort. She knows it's "good enough." She can relax, knowing she's done the best she can with her abilities and skills. She doesn't stop trying to grow, but at the same time she doesn't withhold praise. She can say, "For right now, that's awfully good. I'm pleased, and I know I did the best I could in God's power. Praise the Lord! I'm going to enjoy the fruits of my labor."

Jeanne Zornes, the author of *When I Prayed for Patience, God Let Me Have It!,* told me: "I really think the key to 'healing' perfectionism is differentiating it from the pursuit of excellence. I know I'll never be perfect. But I can still do my best for God. I know life will never be perfect. But I can still creatively work within its boundaries and learn to accept the things I cannot change. I believe perfectionists need to ask (as I have): Will it really matter in terms of eternity? Is it important enough to harm or detract from a relationship? Does this perfectionism stem from spiritual immaturity, or is it a legitimate quest for excellence?"

How can you identify what is "good enough"? I can't answer that for you because it differs from person to person and from task to task. For example, one woman may be satisfied with vacuuming once a day, and another woman once a week. One mom will believe reading to her children for fifteen minutes a day is sufficient, while another enjoys reading for an hour a day. Some projects don't need to be error-free, but others do. A person's "best" often depends upon his or her expertise.

So how can we know if we are striving for excellence or perfection? One way is by our ability to relax and enjoy the moment, whether or not the effort produced perfect results. If we are feeling tense, then we're most likely still focused on striving for perfection. If we are able to relax and trust God—even for mistakes—we are most likely seeking excellence.

Below is a chart that shows the differences between a perfectionist mind-set and an excellence mind-set.

Perfection: Never "Good Enough"	Excellence: "Good Enough"
Judgmental of others and self	Looks for positives in behavior of others or self
Considers life too serious to enjoy fun	Enjoys life through humor
Can't risk delegating responsibility to others	Loves to challenge others with responsibilities and see them grow
Torn in too many directions by lack of priorities	Is able to prioritize the opportunities she receives

Moving Toward Excellence

How can you shift your mind-set from perfection to excellence? Ask God to help you:

Look for the positive. Because we perfectionists have such high—and rigid—standards, we are often judgmental of others and ourselves. As mentioned earlier, we tend to think everyone looks at life the way we do, and we have difficulty understanding why other people don't have standards or goals as high as ours. Yet we overlook the fact that those same high standards—which we are never quite able to attain—are making us tense and angry and are driving others crazy!

As an elementary student, Sarah couldn't spell and had problems with math. However, her reading and vocabulary skills were above grade level, so her teachers told her she was lazy. In high school Sarah would spend five hours typing a two-page paper because she had to look up the spelling of every other word. While she worked hard, she could hear kids outside playing, and she wondered, *What are they doing that I'm not? I should work harder.* She thought of herself as a failure because it took her so long to do everything. Even if a project carried a low priority or had a small effect on her grade, she worked just as hard on it. She felt compelled to do everything perfectly.

In college she finally discovered that her spelling problems were rooted in dyslexia. The psychologist who tested her (who also was dyslexic) asked, "Why do you waste so much effort making sure something is perfect, when it doesn't need to be?"

Sarah was amazed at his comment. In that moment, she understood the difference between perfection and excellence. It helped to set her free. She says, "What a concept! Since then, I ask myself, 'Does this really need to be perfect?' God helps me decide what is really important and what doesn't need to be perfect. As a result, I don't judge myself stupid anymore—or lazy!"

For the remainder of her college career, Sarah could be satisfied with a C grade in those classes that wouldn't impact her life's work. And she concentrated more on attaining As in those subjects that were important for her future job. With her learning disability, she realized she didn't have enough time to get high marks in everything, therefore, she did her best and gave herself credit for working hard. Her self-esteem bloomed and her work improved because she wasn't so stressed.

Whether we are judging ourselves or others with a perfectionist "never good enough" standard, we must remind ourselves there may be extenuating circumstances in others' lives we don't know about. We can look for the positive and say,

"That may be the best that person can do—and that's good enough! That's the best of their abilities. That is excellence for them, even if I could have done it better."

Lighten up! Several years ago I lost a friendship because I took life too seriously. I had met Sylvia at church after she moved to our area. She was depressed that she had to leave her extended family behind, and felt lonely. I encouraged her to share her feelings with me and tried to be a sounding board.

After a while, though, I noticed she wasn't calling me. When we next connected, she explained she was avoiding me on purpose. "Kathy, you always seem to want me to talk about my problems. I need some positives, too."

I had no clue I had been a negative force in her life. Months later, she moved back to her hometown, and I never heard from her again. I regretted losing that friendship because of my inability to lighten up. I was too intense.

We perfectionists need to have more fun! But we're often the ones who have the most difficulty lightening up. Tanya told me, "Learning to laugh at myself has been one of the hardest lessons in my life. After all, life is serious business and my shortcomings are nothing to laugh at. I carried my mistakes, errors, and defects on my shoulders as heavy burdens. I had to learn to take them off my shoulders and hold them out in front of me loosely. Then I could separate my *being* from my *behavior*. Eventually over time, I learned to laugh at my perfectionism."

How wise of Tanya to see that she has a choice to include humor and fun in her life. Laughter is the best medicine: "A cheerful heart is good medicine, but a crushed spirit dries up the bones" (Prv 17:22). Laughing, especially at our inadequacies and mistakes, is a good way to release the "never good enough" woes that can crush our spirit. And if we can treat everything, even difficulties, with a sense of humor, we'll be even farther ahead.

As you make that journey, consider this prayer of a perfectionist and laugh!

Lord, help me to relax about insignificant details beginning tomorrow at 7:41:23 A.M. EST.

Lord, help me to take responsibility for my own actions, even though they're usually not my fault.

Lord, help me to not try to RUN everything, but, if you need some help, please feel free to ask me.

Lord, help me to be more laid back, and help me to do it exactly right.

Lord, give me patience and I mean right NOW!

Lord, help me not be a perfectionist. (Did I spell that correctly?)

Lord, help me to finish everything I sta

Lord, help me to keep my mind on one thing—Look, a bird—at a time.

Lord, help me to do only what I can, and trust you for the rest, and would you mind putting that in writing?

Lord, keep me open to others' ideas, WRONG though they may be.

Lord, help me be less independent, but let me do it my way.

Lord, help me slow down, andnotrushthroughwhatIdo.[2]

Did you laugh? I hope so!

Start delegating. Margaret Houk, author of *Everyday Ways to De-Stress Your Lifestyle*, has learned the hard way about the importance of delegating. She suffered from repeated bouts of stomach trouble, and unknown to her, her stress had reached an overwhelming level. Her family had financial pressures, and her three-year-old daughter was repeatedly ill. Her mind carried her worries to the most extreme degree, and she became clinically depressed.

She told me: "As I recovered, I began to look for factors that had contributed to my ailment. I had seen the stresses building for months and knew I was getting more and more exhausted, but I told myself I could handle it.

"I have a tendency to think I have to do it all. How ridiculous! No one can do everything. My husband could have done his own book work temporarily. Someone else could have taken over my daughter's Girl Scout troop. The reed that bends is less apt to break under pressure. I am now that bendable reed, and I accept and enjoy life more."

Like Margaret, we may need to ask ourselves, "Is there something I can let others do?" If we will risk delegating, we'll have less stress, and other people may grow in their abilities.

I look back and see how I could have delegated more things to my children. Instead, I wanted to do things my way—perfectly—and as a result, they missed out on learning. Whether it was making cookies or calling to make an appointment for a haircut, I often took over. Although they are capable young adults—through God's grace—I wonder whether living those missed experiences might have given them just a bit more confidence.

Perhaps that's why I so enjoyed this humorous but insightful paraphrase of Exodus 18:13-24 that Katherine Bell, author of *Jonathan's Journey*, told me.

One day I was settling disputes between my two-year-old girl and my three-year-old boy, and I was kept busy from morning till night! When my husband saw everything that I had to do, he asked, "What is all this that you are doing for these children?! Why are you doing all this alone when there are high school girls who need your money standing around every afternoon after school, with nothing to do?"

I answered, "I must do this because the children must eat, the shopping must be done, the laundry must be washed, and the bills must be paid! When the children have a dispute, they come to me, and I decide which one of them is right, and I spank the other one."

Then my husband said, "You are not doing this right. You will wear yourself out and these children as well. This is too much for you to do alone. Now let me give you some advice, and God will be with you.

"It is right for you to care for these children. You should teach them God's commands and explain to them how they should live and what they should do. But in addition, you should choose some capable teenage girls and appoint them as helpers for you over the children: leaders of thousands, hundreds, fifties, and tens."

"But, Honey," I said. "We have only two children."

"Really?" he replied. "It looks like more." He continued, "They must be God-fearing girls who can be trusted and who will not beat the children (at least, without cause). Let them serve as helpers for you every Tuesday afternoon after school. They can bring all the difficult cases to you, but they themselves can change a diaper or two. That will make it easier for you as they share your burden. If you do this, as God commands, you will not wear yourself out; and when they are grown, these children will still be able to stand the sight of you."

And I took my husband's advice!

Do you need to do the same? What are some of the responsibilities that you could delegate?

Learn to prioritize your opportunities. An opportunity to do something is not necessarily God's open door. Jesus was given many "opportunities"—opportunities that would bring glory to God—but there were times when he withdrew from the crowds who clamored for him. We're told: "Yet the news about him [Jesus] spread all the more, so that crowds of people came to hear him and to be healed of their sicknesses. But Jesus often withdrew to lonely places and prayed" (Lk 5:15-16). I'm sure some people criticized him for this. Yet he didn't fear people's view or report of him. He knew what his Father wanted him to do, and that's all that mattered.

If we follow Jesus' example, we won't take on more than we can handle. If we know that our priorities are in line with what God wants us to do, we won't worry about how others see us. We'll know we've pleased our Heavenly Father with our efforts—even if they are less than perfect—and that's all that matters.

The next time you are offered an opportunity and you feel compelled to take on an additional task or responsibility, say, "I'll be glad to pray about that and let you know." Then do only what God wants you to do.

A Surprising Response

Are you willing to seek excellence instead of perfection? Are you willing to be satisfied with "good enough" (mistakes and all)? I'm going to close with the following story, praying that it will encourage you to accept your—and other people's—mistakes.

One Christmas Carrie painted sweatshirts to give as gifts. She accidentally spilled some paint on one shirt. She quickly grabbed some water and a sponge and dabbed frantically at the paint. Most of it came out, but a stubborn spot or two remained. Carrie diluted some bleach in water and dabbed at the spots until they came out. Then she dabbed clean water on the places where she'd put the bleach. When the shirt dried, the front looked great, but the back showed the bleached spots because the rinse water hadn't penetrated all the way through.

What should she do? The sweatshirt was ruined. But necessity *is* the mother of invention. Since she couldn't afford to buy another sweatshirt, she painted over the spots on the back, embellishing and adding to them. The end result wasn't what she had envisioned, but she decided it was "good enough" to give to her friend anyway.

Imagine her relief when her friend thanked her for the present and said, "Carrie, I love the shirt you gave me. You are so creative! My favorite part is the unique design on the back that compliments the front design without copying it or borrowing from it."

Carrie told me, "Talk about being flabbergasted—the back was a *mistake!* I guess that just shows how God can turn things around when you least expect them to become blessings! It also taught me how to ease up on myself (a little)."

I love this story! It's ironic that what Carrie considered a mistake, her friend considered creative. If Carrie had thrown away the sweatshirt and spent money she didn't have, she would have gone into debt and missed out on God's surprise blessing. Let's take the lesson in Carrie's story to heart and be satisfied with "good enough."

∿

Eight

Why Can't People Get Their Act Together?

I couldn't understand why Larry didn't relate to our eleven-year-old son the way I did. Didn't he know he was discouraging Mark with his "just do it" responses? *Can't he see that Mark needs his dad to be sensitive and caring? They seem so opposite, but if Larry would reach out to Mark, I know it would give Mark more confidence in spite of his learning disability. If Larry would just do what I say, their relationship would be great.*

I'd repeatedly talked to Larry and cried out to God. "After all, I'm right! Why can't Larry see it? He keeps insisting he *is* being a loving father to Mark, but if he would just do more loving, sensitive things, Mark wouldn't feel so bad about himself." Over and over I prayed for Larry to see things my way. When God didn't change Larry's mind, I wondered, "God, do you really know best? Lord, please work!"

One evening as I drove home from Bible study, I'd had enough. All my frustration and pleadings had gotten us nowhere. "God, why don't you do anything? Mark needs a more sensitive father." Through my angry tears, I could barely see to drive. "Make Larry hear me!"

Suddenly the Lord whispered in my heart, "Praise me!"

"Lord, I don't feel like praising you. I'm too mad."

"Praise me!" he repeated.

I didn't feel like it, but I knew God was more interested in my choices than my feelings. I began singing a praise chorus even though my heart was not in it. But the more I sang, the stronger my voice became, and the more my frustration dissipated. By the time I reached the end of the song, I knew I could trust God again—even if he didn't make Larry do what I wanted. "All right, Lord, I give up. I acknowledge I don't know everything, and I'll trust that you know the best thing to do about Larry and Mark's relationship." My heart was at peace. I reminded myself of truth: I can't control anyone else. Only God can.

Moments later I arrived home. After getting ready for bed, I slipped between the sheets beside Larry in the darkened bedroom. As I lay there, Larry suddenly spoke up and said, "I was thinking on the way home from work about doing something with Mark. Do you think he would like to learn to play golf so that we can play together?"

Oh, Lord, thank you! I silently prayed. "I think that's a great idea, Honey. Yes, be sure to mention it to him."

The two of them have enjoyed many rounds of golf together since then. God answered my prayer in his way and in his time.

Perfectionists believe they know what other people should do and be. As a result, we are often critical of others, thinking, *Why can't they get their act together?* We believe that if the significant people in our lives would just do what we know is best, then we'd be happy and not have any problems! "Perfectionists can actually feel superior because of their high standards. Their own sense of fairness, justice, and duty leads them to believe that everyone should act as they do."[1]

Leanne is a self-proclaimed perfectionist who scored an "eleven and a half" on the quiz at the beginning of this book. She told me, "I'm often frustrated because other people are so incompetent even after I instruct them on how to get it right! Yet, I'm realizing that this attitude is destructive to relationships. It robs me of peace of mind. It establishes expectations that cannot and should not be met. Even more important, it distracts me from what is truly important: people."

Leanne has grown in her ability to handle her perfectionist expectations of the people around her, and we can too.

Understanding Why People Act the Way They Do

Why can't people get their act together? Because people are human. We're all mistake-prone and sinful. We'll never get all the puzzle pieces of our *own* lives into the correct order, yet we still get frustrated with other people whose pieces are helter-skelter on the game table.

It's also true that *different isn't wrong.* Although we may believe our way is the best way—the *only* way—to do something, this is NOT true. God made each of us unique, and we each come with a different set of preferences. One is not necessarily better than the other.

This became clear to me in 1977 when I began reading *Understanding the Male Temperament* by Tim LaHaye. Until then I had assumed Larry and I looked at life in the same way. In other words, I believed:

- What was important to me should be important to him, and
- I could interpret what he meant by his actions and didn't have to ask him.

When Larry's actions didn't match these expectations, I became hurt and angry. I knew I needed help understanding him better. While browsing in the bookstore one day, the title of Tim LaHaye's book caught my attention. I bought the book expectantly and found the information about personality styles so helpful that I read everything I could on the subject. How wrong I had been! Larry and I aren't the same at all; Larry looks at life differently than I do.

When we understand the different temperaments—or learning styles, as some call them—we can become more patient, loving, and kind toward people who approach life differently than we do. We'll be less likely to require people to do things our way, and we'll be more gentle toward ourselves as well. At least that has been the case for me.

Trudie had picked me up at the airport in order to transport me to the conference center where I would be speaking for her church's women's retreat. She was the pastor's wife, and as we talked we discovered we both had studied the different personality temperaments. I told her I am an Analytical, and as I had suspected from her easygoing manner, she told me she was an Amiable. (We will identify the four temperaments in a moment.)

When we arrived at the conference center, I left my speaking materials and visual aids in the car. Fifteen or so minutes before the first session was to start, I reminded Trudie that I needed to get my material out of her car. But as we started walking across the conference center on the way to the car, numerous women stopped Trudie to talk with her—and she talked with each one! I started to get nervous, thinking that I wouldn't have any time to arrange my notes and visual aids. (I had spent hours preparing for my talk, and I wanted it to go smoothly.) Also, I was hurt and irritated that Trudie didn't seem to be concerned about me and what I needed.

Then I remembered what I knew about Trudie's temperament. As a nonassertive Amiable, she wanted peace and she didn't want to rock the boat. That made it difficult for her to tell these women, "I'm sorry, I can't talk right now. I've got to help our speaker get her materials." Remembering this enabled me to avoid taking her behavior personally. It also reminded me that my nervousness stemmed from my perfectionism. I had no reason to be nervous about not being ready. I *was* ready; I had arranged all my material and aids prior to leaving home! I took a deep breath and silently prayed for God's grace to relax. Of course, we made it to the car in time and I was prepared when I was called to the platform to speak.

This is only one of a number of personal illustrations I could give for how understanding personality types can help us accept others as well as ourselves.

What Are the Four Temperaments?

I created the following chart to summarize the differences among the four basic temperaments.[2]

	Expressive	Driver	Analytical	Amiable
Basic Desire	Wants fun	Wants to control	Wants perfection	Wants peace at any cost
Strengths	Friendly and talkative Has a good sense of humor Creative and and charming Energetic and restless Thrives on compliments	Dynamic leader Sees big picture Determined to succeed Quick thinker Independent	Conscientious Loves to think and analyze Appreciates culture and the arts Thorough and organized Loves details Good listener and loyal friend Compassionate	Easy-going and calm Quick wit Excellent mediator Compassionate, listens patiently More a watcher than a doer
Weaknesses	Exaggerates what he or she says Undisciplined in organization and behavior Craves approval, attention, and applause	Unemotional and doesn't value emotions Domineering, believing he or she knows best Lacks empathy for others' hurts Intolerant of the weaknesses of others	Perfectionist Easily depressed Remembers hurts and readily becomes resentful Unrealistic expectations of others and self Has a hard time being flexible	Low awareness of own emotions Low energy level Easily worries Lacks self-motivation Loves to tease

Let's look at the different personalities in context.

Erika has an Expressive personality, and she loves to engage in all kinds of activities so that she can be with friends *or* strangers—it doesn't matter. Of course, she'll have the best time if she can entertain everyone with her quick wit and lively stories. Erika much prefers to be with friends or family rather than by herself. When she is by herself, organizing or cleaning her house, she often calls a friend on the telephone rather than working toward her cleaning goals for the day. Erika is great in jobs that require relating to people, especially sales positions. But disciplining her children isn't "fun"; she'd rather play with her children instead.

Lucy is a typical Driver. She is goal-oriented at work, much preferring to delegate responsibilities to others, although she's good at carrying out projects herself. In working with co-workers or as the manager of employees, she demands efficiency and expects a lot from herself too. When asked her opinion, she has no trouble giving it, and she rarely second-guesses her decisions. If there's a need for leadership at work or in an organization, she'll quickly step in and take over. Because by nature she has such a high opinion of her own abilities, she has a hard time depending on the Holy Spirit's control. She considers her own plans quite appropriate and therefore tends to be dependent upon herself rather than on God or others. She can sure get a job done, though!

Cassie hasn't always appreciated her Analytical temperament because in her drive for perfection, she thinks becoming like someone else would bring her greater happiness. She tends to be introspective and loves facts and details—so much so that she gets bogged down by "analysis paralysis." Making decisions becomes difficult for her because she's always thinking there could be more facts she hasn't yet discovered. Even though she views life seriously, she can be a good friend because she is sensitive to the needs and feelings of others. But that sensitivity can cause her to be easily offended by others and prone to moodiness.

Lauren is a natural Amiable and doesn't mind at all that she doesn't have strong opinions about things. She is perfectly at ease letting others make decisions or have their own way. That's because she wants peace—sometimes at any cost. A part of her temperament is looking at life with rose-colored glasses and seeing the good side of everyone and everything—anything to avoid confrontation or making others angry. But this God-given characteristic has its benefits, for she is effective at bringing warring parties together and helping them find a compromise.

Understanding What Motivates People

As I studied the temperaments or learning styles, I discovered that each of us has a mixture of these personality traits. However, one set of characteristics is more evident than others, and when we are under stress, we tend to operate out of our dominant temperament. When we are not under stress, we are more capable of choosing to behave in another way that may be more appropriate for the situation—and that's good. That's called "versatility," the ability to behave with the strengths of another temperament in the Holy Spirit's power. But when we're under stress, we tend to revert back to our fundamental viewpoint—unless we choose to be versatile with God's help.

For instance, as an Analytical personality (and you already know I'm a perfectionist!) I find it hard to be flexible. For me, flexibility means working on several different projects in a day. That's hard for me. With my "all or nothing" characteristic, I want to concentrate on one writing project at a time. When I'm not facing a deadline, I may find it easier to stop concentrating on one project and turn my attention to something else that needs to be done. But when I'm under a deadline, and two people are expecting two different things from me, my stress level deepens and I don't want to vacillate between the two projects. Even at the risk of being late on a project, I might focus solely on one. The only solution is to ask God for help and trust he can give me the ability to be flexible. That is the solution for all of us as we deal with the weaknesses of our own temperaments and the weaknesses of others.

According to Rose Sweet, a certified personality trainer and author of *How to Be First in a Second Marriage*, each personality avoids rejection differently. She told me, "Fear of rejection is the main cause of our weaknesses, no matter our personality, but each temperament avoids rejection in different ways. Expressives charm, Drivers threaten anger, Amiables withdraw or procrastinate, and Analyticals use perfectionism. Knowing that, I can look with compassion on those who hold unrealistically high standards for themselves and for me. I realize they are just seeking acceptance, trying to avoid rejection, and have not yet come to love themselves on the same level God does!"

This insight is important: when someone doesn't behave or perform as we expected or would like, we may be quick to think, "Why can't they get their act together?" Or, "They sure are incompetent." But instead, we can remind ourselves about the temperaments and ask ourselves: "What need is that person trying to fulfill by reacting that way?" Or, "What is it within that person's temperament that creates a need to act that way?" We may not always be able to figure it out (and even if we do, we could be wrong unless the person has told us), but by seeing the potential inner needs, we'll be more understanding.

This knowledge has helped me change my perspective about Larry and Mark's relationship. Larry, a Driver, is goal-oriented and makes fast decisions. He loves conflict (he's a policeman!). But Mark, an Amiable, lives at a relaxed pace and avoids conflict. Larry tries to understand Mark's core nature, but he sees life through a different set of lenses. And as for me, an Analytical, I want my husband and son to have a perfect relationship!

Over the years, Larry has become more sensitive and compassionate, Mark has become more productive and motivated, and I've stopped pressuring Larry to parent like me. We've all become more versatile. We don't as often think of each other as incompetent, only that we each have different views of life.

Is there someone who frustrates you because you think they "can't get their act together"? Could it be because each of you defines "act" differently? Do you have goals and basic desires that are at odds with each other? Are there different motives energizing you and others?

Become More Versatile

Let's look at some scenarios of different relationships and see how we can become more versatile in accepting other people's temperament faults and weaknesses.

Sarah is a Driver perfectionist married to Allan, an Expressive. Sarah tells Allan, "Honey, I need to get the kitchen cleaned up, so please help Johnny pick up his toys in his room. The Chandlers are coming over tonight for dessert, and I want Johnny's room to be clean so he can play with their son."

Sarah is busy in the kitchen when she hears hysterical giggles from Johnny's room. Feeling tense about having company, she walks down the hall toward the room. She arrives to see Allan lying on the floor, throwing plastic building blocks up into the air as Johnny jumps up and down in delight.

In a fit of frustration, Sarah throws down her kitchen towel and mutters, "Why can't he value our reputation and teach his child organization skills?"

* * *

Jackie is a Driver perfectionist and the director of women's ministries at her church. Currently she is mentoring Linda, who is an Amiable, in setting up the mother-daughter event for the next year. Jackie recently called Linda and asked, "Have you found someone to do the table decorations?"

"Well, two women want to do it and they're both capable. I suggested they do it together, but they didn't like that idea."

Jackie replied, "Linda, you're in charge here. Just go ahead and pick one of them."

"But one of them might feel left out."

"That's one of the risks of leadership. It's their responsibility how they react, not yours."

"Well, I'll try, but they're both so good. How will I choose?"

About this time, Jackie was holding her head in her hands in frustration. She wanted to scream, "Take charge and do it right!"

* * *

Joyce, an Analytical perfectionist, is a friend of Lizzy, who is a Driver. As two single women, they recently planned a week-long trip together driving up the coast of California. On their first day, Lizzy drove and Joyce kept pointing out the sights of interest, thinking this communicated that she wanted to stop and visit each one—her definition of the *perfect* vacation. She fumed, "Why doesn't Lizzy want to stop? A vacation is supposed to be relaxing and enjoyable, with lots of visits at interesting places."

But as a Driver who was in control of the car, Lizzy just wanted to arrive at their destination as quickly as possible. Her definition of vacation was arriving, not the process of traveling. By the time they arrived at their motel—five hours earlier than their itinerary called for—Joyce was fit to be tied. She just wanted to go home. She fumed, "Obviously, Lizzy doesn't really care about me at all. Otherwise she would have cared about my opinion."

Each of these examples illustrates how a person's temperamental weaknesses can drive a perfectionist crazy. There is even conflict when an Analytical perfectionist interacts with another Analytical perfectionist because each has her own ideas of what perfection means. For instance, Kelly and Amy are working on the same project at work, but Kelly regards one area as more deserving of extended research, while Amy considers another area important. They don't have the time or resources to concentrate on both, so they are unhappy, each believing her opinion is the right one.

Everyone looks at life through the filter of his or her temperament and has trouble seeing life any other way. If we want to be more accepting of others, and less critical and judgmental, we need to act more out of our strengths than our weaknesses. We need to learn to operate in the power of the Holy Spirit. With his help we can become more versatile and grow in our understanding of others.

As we become familiar with the strengths and weaknesses of our loved ones' temperaments, we can offer them grace. A couple was celebrating their fiftieth wedding anniversary and a relative asked the wife her secret for a long and happy marriage. She replied, "When we got married I decided to list ten of my husband's faults to ignore." The inquiring relative was anxious to know what those ten faults were. The older woman said, "Oh, I never wrote them down! Every time he did something I didn't like, I just said to myself, 'Good thing that's one of the ten!' and then ignored it."

The Most Important Key: Release and Trust God

If we want to give up our desire to control other people's behavior and thus become more versatile, it's essential that we trust God to work in others and change them as he wills. If you are like me, you sometimes act as if you know better than God what others need. Instead, we can rely on the Holy Spirit to work from the inside out; he is much more effective than we are when we try to pressure them from the outside. Nagging, manipulation, and other kinds of control just don't compare to the ability of God's Spirit to bring change.

That may be one of the messages Jesus wanted to communicate in his response to Martha in Luke 10:38-42:

As Jesus and his disciples were on their way, he came to a village where a woman named Martha opened her home to him. She had a sister called Mary, who sat at the Lord's feet listening to what he said. But Martha was distracted by all the preparations that had to be made. She came to him and asked, "Lord, don't you care that my sister has left me to do the work by myself? Tell her to help me!"

"Martha, Martha," the Lord answered, "you are worried and upset about many things, but only one thing is needed. Mary has chosen what is better, and it will not be taken away from her."

Martha wanted Mary to "get her act together." She wanted Mary to do what she would do! You and I do that when we:

- Dictate to our husband how to respond to our child
- Try to control the response of our boss toward our co-worker
- Encourage our daughter to do better in school by comparing her to a friend or sibling
- Give advice to an independent adult child without their asking
- Tell a friend what to do before getting the whole story and hearing her feelings
- Share with a mutual friend what a friend should do about something, hoping the mutual friend will pass it along
- Instruct our adult child and his or her spouse how to discipline our grandchild without being asked for advice
- Take over responsibility for something that the committee chairperson hasn't given to us
- Call the pastor to suggest that he tell your friend how to deal with her problem.

What did Jesus say to Martha? "Martha, you take care of yourself, and I'll take care of Mary. You're hot and bothered trying to get everything done when one thing would suffice. [Did he mean: things don't need to be perfect?] Martha has chosen the best thing, time with me. I won't take that away from her, and I wouldn't take it away from you if you chose it."

He says the same thing to you and me. "You take care of you, and I'll take care of them. Just be concerned about walking close to me, and then you'll know that I have everything else under control."

Yet some of us still think, *Lord, what I want really is best for them.* We don't like to hear it, but when we think we know better than God, we're being selfish and proud. We're trying to play the role of the Holy Spirit! Author David Seamands says it this way, "The performance-based Christian life comes from the malignant virus of sinful pride—a pride which encourages us to build our lives upon a deadly lie. This lie claims that everything depends on what we do and on how well we perform, on our efforts and our work."[3] The lie also says that the people we interact with are a reflection of us! And our pride doesn't want anyone to think poorly of us as a result of someone else's behavior.

Trying to control others means we believe God can't control the universe. Trying to force people to agree with us means we believe God can't change people's minds if that's what he wants. Trying to manipulate someone to think a certain way means we don't believe God can bring about circumstances to influence a person's thinking.

God is in control; he can do anything he wants. We just have to trust and believe. We can have the attitude of Daniel when he said,

Praise be to the name of God for ever and ever; wisdom and power are his. He changes times and seasons; he sets up kings and deposes them. He gives wisdom to the wise and knowledge to the discerning. He reveals deep and hidden things; he knows what lies in darkness, and light dwells with him. I thank and praise you, O God of my fathers: You have given me wisdom and power, you have made known to me what we asked of you, you have made known to us the dream of the king.

DANIEL 2:20-23

Let's Remember...

Sarah, Jackie, Joyce, Kelly, and Amy—any one of the perfectionists in the scenarios we saw earlier—could trust God and respond in a godly way by remembering a few key guidelines:

- The "transgressing" person wasn't annoying her on purpose. It was that person's temperament—the perspective of life given to him or her by God—that created the irritation. By not taking the behavior personally, as if that person intended to annoy her, she will be able to relax and not regard the other person as "incompetent."
- Different isn't necessarily wrong. There are many ways of doing things. Unless an action is in direct disobedience to God's Word, then it could be just one of several ways to accomplish a task or respond to a situation.
- We all make mistakes and grow through them. We can choose to be gracious, knowing that God is working in that person, even as we share our perspective with them. We

can't force anyone to change, but we can trust God to work 1 percent at a time in someone's life as we offer our ideas.

Finally, we can relax because the behavior we're calling "incompetent" might be the very behavior we will exhibit at another time—even moments later. We've all yelled at the driver who cut us off and then cut someone else off before we got home. We've all gotten frustrated with someone who can't see the reason for something and then encountered someone hours later who says we don't have common sense about something else. None of us are perfect. None of us are totally competent. None of us have our act together. As soon as we criticize someone else, God may humble us by putting us into a situation where we fall into a similar trap. Just listen to Roseanne's story.

Roseanne often looked at some people's "insensitivity" to others and secretly thought, *Whew, I'm glad sensitivity is my strong point, and I'm surely glad I am not like them. They should get their act together!*

But one day she fell into a trap. She needed to call a man at her church who was deeply loved by everyone, but he stuttered. As she dialed his number, she told herself, "Roseanne, whatever you do, do not stutter." She had never stuttered, but she was aware that others had teased this man about his stutter, and she had felt they were insensitive and cruel. She was determined not to do the same.

Roseanne dialed and heard Rusty's answering machine. When the beep sounded, she blurted out, "R-R-R—Rusty this is R-R-R—Roseanne. Please C-C-C—Call me back."

Roseanne couldn't believe what had happened. She wanted to die! Her husband watched the whole thing and said, "That was the cruelest thing I have *ever* seen you do."

On the verge of tears, she called one of her friends to get some comfort. But all her friend could do was laugh hysterically. Then she called her pastor, but he was on the floor in stitches too. By the time church rolled around the next day, everyone had heard about it. They all decided to play a joke on her, and after church everyone was in the back, waiting to see what would happen.

Rusty was in on the joke and approached her, looking very sad. He said he would like to talk to her about something. Roseanne thought, *Oh, great, Lord. Just kill me now.*

Rusty said, "I'm disss...apppp...ointed in you and your insensitivity. I cccan't believe that someone with your spiritual maturity could be so cruel."

Roseanne was on the verge of tears—and then she heard the snickers. All her friends were looking on, and then Rusty burst out laughing. Roseanne learned a lesson that day. She told me: "I know better now than to think I am 'above' doing things I see others doing. If I start to catch myself thinking that way, I think about Rusty and I quickly repent."

Take heed: As soon as we look down on someone for not "getting *their* act together," we should think of the times when we couldn't even *find* our "act." Then we can remind ourselves, "There, but for the grace of God, go I!"

Nine

I'm Compelled to Straighten Out Misunderstandings

I hung up the phone and suddenly felt uncomfortable about something I'd said. *Why did I make that comment about her working even though her children were in elementary school?* I racked my brain, trying to remember my exact words. I hadn't meant anything derogatory about working moms, but would she take it that way? Especially since I'd also said that I hadn't worked when my children were young. *Oh, no! Put the two comments together and what did she think?*

And after I said that, she was silent. Is she unhappy? Hurt? Or was she just distracted by her kids? Oh, I wish I knew. I bet she hates me now. She's most likely calling Sheila and telling her how I put her down for working. Now Sheila will hate me too. Oh, if only I hadn't said that! Why did I say that?

Should I call and apologize? But what if she didn't take it wrong? Will my apology just make her think about my comments—and then she'll be hurt?

I worried over our conversation the rest of the day. *Should I call and explain?* I didn't know what to do, and consequently felt edgy and tense.

Have you ever had similar conversations in your mind? Most women place a high priority on their relationships and are sensitive to how others feel. This is particularly true of the perfectionist. The perfectionist "focuses on someone's body language or tone of voice or some other subtle behavior as evidence of a negative attitude toward them. No matter what, they are able to find some reason to think other people feel negative about them. In reality, they are attributing their own negative feelings about themselves to other people."[1]

If a perfectionist believes there has been a misunderstanding, she can't think about anything else until the problem is fixed. Now, this trait isn't always bad or to be avoided. Jesus told us to right wrongs when we've offended anyone or sinned against them (see Mt 5:23-24). That's good sense, and it shows humility and a teachable spirit. It's also obedience!

But unfortunately, perfectionists overdo it. Our emotional antennae are alert to anything that sounds like someone is upset with us. Even without evidence that we've offended someone, we will imagine we have. We can't stand the thought that someone could be irritated or unhappy with us because we want her approval—and we want everyone to be happy. (That's our definition of a "perfect" relationship.)

But such a goal is misdirected. Even Jesus didn't make everyone happy: he was concerned about pleasing only his Father. He said, "By myself I can do nothing; I judge only as I hear, and my judgment is just, for I seek not to please myself but him who sent me" (Jn 5:30). The Pharisees misunderstood Jesus' mission, yet he didn't give a second thought to convincing them of his intentions. Jesus knew the truth: every person is responsible for his or her own happiness. Even though Jesus was perfect in every way, people still were angry, critical, and unhappy about his choices and priorities. He knew the Pharisees wanted him to fulfill their agenda, not the Father's. Nothing he could say or do would please them.

We Aren't Responsible for Another Person's Happiness

For years Dottie believed that she had the power to make her mother happy. An alcoholic, Dottie's mother was temperamental, verbally abusive, and inconsistent, yet Dottie kept trying to smooth out the conflicts in their relationship. After her parents divorced and her mom remarried, Dottie tried to diffuse her mother's mood swings by keeping the house clean, rubbing her back, and fixing dinner. But it never worked. Her mom complained, "Nobody wants to be around someone who is bossy and who talks constantly, like you, Dottie. Your pediatrician told me to stay on top of your strong will, and I will if it kills me."

Dottie thought, *Wait, what did I do? I try not to act silly or talk all the time, but you are still angry. You're mean. I hate you.... Well, not really, but please don't tell the doctor lies about me. I'll do better. Give me another chance, I'll be good again.* Dottie kept trying to gain her mother's approval.

Over the years, her mom would scream at her, "It's no use, we will never get along, so why even try...." That was Dottie's hot button. She would beg, "I can get along! Please, *please,* give me one more chance. I'll prove I can!"

As soon as Dottie said those words, her mom would smile. Then Dottie would berate herself. *Why do I let her do this to me? Great! Now she will be mad at me for days until I crawl back and say I'm sorry for ... what ... trying my best? Why can't I just let her stay mad at me?*

Tears soaked Dottie's face. She swallowed hard. "I'm sorry, Mom."

When Dottie was a college student, God used all that conflict to show her her need of a relationship with him. She says, "How could I turn down God's unconditional love? I had yearned for acceptance my whole life." Although much healing occurred at that time, she still felt compelled to fix her relationship with her mom.

This pattern continued until Dottie's mom died of lung cancer when Dottie was thirty-three. By that time, her mom had disowned her and refused to allow her to visit her in the hospital as she lay dying. After much emotional healing, Dottie knows now that she could never please her mother or make her happy. Her mother refused to find happiness within herself, therefore Dottie wasn't going to be able to force her mother to be happy.

Are you like Dottie? Are there people in your life who refuse to accept your efforts to make them happy? Do they refuse to cooperate with healing a misunderstanding? Romans 12:18 gives us God's perspective: "If it is possible, as far as it depends on you, live at peace with everyone." God says that you can only do what you can do. Even after trying to make relationships right and clearing up misunderstandings, you may not be successful. If so, you don't need to feel guilty or burdened. You can't change anyone else or force anyone to love you, be your friend, or approve of you. Yet God wants to be and do all those things for you.

Releasing the Compulsion

If this chapter strikes a chord in your heart, there are some things you can do.

Evaluate. In order to determine whether you're being overly sensitive to an obvious or perceived misunderstanding, ask yourself these questions after praying for discernment:

- How much is there to lose if I do nothing?
- How important is this person to me?
- How important is this incident to me?
- How much pain am I in about this?

If you respond with answers like "much" or "lots," then take action. If your responses are "a little" or "insignificant," try to release your anxiety.

Regardless of your responses to these questions, if God is telling you to take action, then do it. But it could be that your perfectionism is directing you rather than God. Asking counsel from an objective person may help you discern God's voice from your own voice.

Ask God to help you become less concerned about what others think and more concerned about what he thinks. Perfectionists have such a strong need for approval that it's tough to stop caring about what others think of us. We want others to see us as perfectly nice, perfectly poised, perfectly together. It can be hard to change our focus from "What do they think of me?" to "What does God think of me?" Sometimes it may even seem easier to be concerned about what others think of us because we can hide our true self from people, but we can't hide from God. Therefore, focusing on others' opinions keeps us insulated from facing the truth about God's opinion of us.

But our loving, sovereign God already knows us completely. He sent Jesus to die for us anyway, and he accepts us without a single *"When you become* _____ (you choose your "hot button": sinless, free of anger, empty of selfishness, clean from bad thoughts), *then I'll love you."* Why wouldn't we want to be more concerned about such a wonderful, loving God? So let's, first of all, be honest before him and seek his opinion.

Little by little we can learn to turn our attention from others to God. It won't be easy, but each time we feel tense about someone's opinion and can identify that we are overly concerned about that individual's perspective of us, then we can make a choice to focus on God. "Lord, what do you think of me in this situation? You see my heart; that friend doesn't. You know my motives; that family member can't. I want your opinion." Chances are, the tension may not dissipate quickly, but each time we "fix our eyes on Jesus, the author and perfecter of our faith" (Heb 12:2), the difficulty of doing that will lessen.

As a speaker, I am often given the opportunity to read the evaluation sheets at the end of a retreat when I speak. Once in a while, someone will write a scathing comment about me. As I read it, it's like a dagger in my heart. I want to find the person and try to correct her opinion of me.

Since I know I can't do that, it takes God's power within me to release my heart and the need to defend myself. At such times I have to pray, "Lord, I can't change anyone's opinion of me. If you are unhappy with the way I served you, let me know. But if I have pleased you, I don't need to please anyone else."

God can guide us in knowing how we should respond to misunderstandings or conflicts. He knows everything, but that friend or family member can't know our heart. We should do as much as God says to do, but there may come the time when he says, "Enough is enough."

Release what you can't change. Jerri is learning this. She says, "As a minister's wife, I waste a lot of valuable time and mental energy going over how I can improve things and make sure everyone is hearing things correctly. My husband is a man of few words, so I feel compelled to follow up on him to make sure he's been understood."

What does Jerri do to fight these urges? "I'm learning to be content with everything! Plus, I'm biting my tongue and sitting on my hands more often!"

To help you release what you can't change, Dr. Kevin Leman suggests you write out a list of the things you are responsible for and the things you aren't.[2]

For example:

- Are you responsible for your husband's irritation about his work situation? You may feel like you should apologize for it, but you aren't actually responsible.
- Are you responsible for your son's room mother forgetting to bring snacks even though you reminded her? Release it.
- Are you responsible for the weather that spoiled the family reunion? Release it.
- Are you responsible for snapping at your neighbor when she ran into your car? Yes! Apologize.

- Are you responsible for being disgruntled and complaining when your friend was chosen to give the devotional at your mothers' group when you wanted to do it? Yes! Apologize.

Now take some time to write out your list.

You are accountable only for the things you can control or you can choose. Release everything else. This may not be easy in the beginning, but 1 percent at a time, you will feel more comfortable as you go along.

Trust that God can bring good out of misunderstandings. Although God doesn't design or desire that misunderstandings happen, he can—and does—use them. When Paul and Barnabas disagreed about whether John Mark should join them on their next missionary journey, each felt he was right and that the other person didn't understand his perspective. They disagreed so sharply that they went in different directions (see Acts 15:36-41). God used it to double the effectiveness of their efforts.

Carol Kent, author and founder of *Speak Up With Confidence,* saw firsthand how God uses conflict. In the past, she had tried to clear up every potential misunderstanding. But she faced a challenge when she was involved in a Christian organization that had a change in leadership. The new leadership determined that she couldn't speak other than for their organization. Since she didn't agree with their new directive, she felt compelled to write a multiple-page letter to the chairperson, explaining all the reasons she should be allowed to speak both inside and outside the organization.

Today Carol realizes that she should have just accepted their decision as God's direction for resigning. But at the time, she wanted to straighten out what she perceived as their incorrect and unfair thinking. She says, "I could have saved myself an enormous amount of energy. As I resigned from that organization and expanded my own personal ministry of speaking, I saw God bless in ways I never expected. If I hadn't released changing them, I might still be there. Instead I enjoy a broadly based ministry which brings great results for the Lord."

There are times when God is working through misunderstandings and we need to cooperate, not fight. If we trust him, we'll let go.

This is the basis for everything, isn't it?

So often we agonize over a misunderstanding or a break in a relationship because we want to know "why?" We wonder if we could have done something differently. We re-create the breakup in our minds, trying to make it come out another way. These mental gyrations only increase our frustration and enslave us to thinking about the situation.

But God tells us, "Let go, and let me take charge. Trust that I know what I want to do in your life and in your friend. You don't have to have a relationship with that person in order to be whole or loved. I already love you unconditionally."

Let God be the judge. The apostle Paul said in 1 Thessalonians 2:4, "We are not trying to please men but God, who tests our hearts." When we know God understands the intentions of our hearts, and still loves and accepts us, we can stop trying to explain our motives to everyone else or clear up every misunderstanding. Even if we explain the reason for our comment or behavior, we have no guarantee that the person will change his or her mind and understand. We should make every effort to "live at peace with everyone" (Rom 12:18), but only God can truly understand our heart.

Billy Graham is highly respected by Christians and unbelievers alike. Yet, he has faced criticism and misunderstandings. Graham's approach to misunderstandings can be seen in an article he wrote in 1960 titled "What Ten Years Have Taught Me."

> It was just ten years ago that my evangelistic work came to the attention of the church as the result of a Los Angeles crusade. To me it was like a bolt of lightning out of a clear sky.... I found my sermons and statements being analyzed and criticized by hundreds of clergy, laymen, and theologians throughout the world. Religious periodicals joined in applause or criticism on my message, methods, and motives. To say the least, I was baffled ... and even frightened.
>
> Over and over again I went to my knees for guidance and direction.... There have been triumphs and defeats, elations and deflations, but never once have I doubted the validity of the gift or the call to evangelism.[3]

When we are misunderstood, we should honestly face our own weaknesses and mistakes. And we must seek God's face for any needed corrections—also for his confirmation of the ways we are obeying him. We can explain ourselves to others as God directs, but we need not always surrender to our perfectionist tendencies to straighten out misunderstandings or feel responsible for the attitudes of others.

By the way, are you still wondering whether I called the friend I mentioned in this chapter's opening? I did call her. She told me she couldn't remember what was said and certainly hadn't been offended. She appreciated my concern. After I hung up, I began thinking about what we'd said and wondered if she *now* was offended. *Oh, no, now she's really going to hate me....*

OK, I'm teasing you. I refused to rehearse the conversation again. See? I am learning something. So are you! We will conquer this perfectionism yet ... perfectly, right?

Ten

~

I Won't Begin Something If I Can't Do It Well

Have you ever hesitated to begin something because you wondered whether you would be pleased when it was finished? Have you felt tense thinking of a project because you were afraid your boss wouldn't be happy with the result? Do you delay starting your housecleaning until you have a significant amount of time to work on it?

Perfectionists don't like starting something if we can't do it well. Listen to what women have told me about how this tendency affects them.

My perfectionism keeps me from completing projects. It also keeps me from doing things I enjoy. For example, I love to sew. But I will not start a project unless the house is clean and I can sit down without any chores bugging me. I always say I'll start exercising, but unless I know I can make the commitment, I keep putting it off. It even affects my willingness to witness. I don't share my faith because I feel my life needs to be perfect before I can.

* * *

I put things off because I don't ever feel like I "measure up" to anyone else. I constantly criticize myself. I think some-

times I'm afraid to do well, or maybe it's that I'm so afraid
I will fail that I defeat myself before it happens.

* * *

I like a clean house, but I don't like to clean it unless I know
that I can clean every room in one time period. And it must
look like picture-perfect when I'm through. Consequently
my house stays messy a lot!

Can you relate? I sure can! It's only an hour until I'll have
to leave for a meeting and as I thought about starting this
chapter, I mused, *But I don't have enough time to complete it, so
I might as well not start it until tomorrow!* Then I reminded
myself of the topic of this chapter....

What to do?

Many people believe that perfectionists (of all people)
should be more successful than most. After all, aren't they the
ones who are motivated to get it done right?

Actually, studies show that's not true. Psychologist David
Burns conducted a study on thirty-four highly successful insurance agents. Burns asked each businessman to score himself on
a Perfectionism Scale. Eighteen identified themselves as perfectionists; the other sixteen considered themselves to be nonperfectionist. He also administered a second questionnaire that
assessed the tendency to measure personal worth and self-
esteem by success and productivity. He writes:

> I anticipated that the highest salaries would be earned by
> those who were perfectionists and most likely to evaluate
> their self-esteem in terms of sales.
>
> The results were surprising. The average earnings of the
> perfectionists were not significantly greater than that of the

nonperfectionists. In fact, the trend was in the opposite direction; the perfectionists who linked self-worth and achievement earned an average of $15,000 a year less than the nonperfectionists did. Apparently the salesmen who were striving for perfection were actually paying a price in dollars for their mental habit.[1]

Burns goes on to indicate that perfectionists tend to set goals that are too high and then become fearful about trying to meet them. He says the results of the insurance salesmen's study is confirmed by studies of successful athletes and students. In all these studies, perfectionists weren't as successful because their mental images of self-doubt and impending tragedy create a fear of failure. Perfectionists are paralyzed by that fear of failure. As a result, we feel tense. Our hearts start to pound. We find other things to do. We think of all the obstacles. We review our past failures. And we convince ourselves, "I'll work on that tomorrow." Or, "I'll make that sales call tomorrow." Or, "I'll clean the house tomorrow."

A writer friend of mine knows all about this. She wrote me, saying, "When I'm writing an article, I'll labor over every paragraph for months before I'll submit it anywhere. I'm forever thinking that if I wait one more day, I'll find the perfect clipping or quote to add or I'll find a glaring error that I would have missed had I sent it out sooner."

Contributions to the Fear of Failure

What makes us so afraid to fail? Here are some classic patterns of perfectionist thinking:

Incorrectly defining success and failure. Perfectionists are black and white when it comes to defining success or failure. We think success equals perfection, and failure equals anything less than perfection. For instance, we set goals for success such as: "Everyone I contact must result in a sale for the day to be successful." Or, "The floor must stay completely clean for the whole day after I wash it—even if I have preschoolers." Or, "The children in my class must all get an A if I've taught that module effectively."

Downplaying our successes and highlighting our failures. I encounter this continually as I talk with women. One woman told me, "I'm able to spend less time in bed due to my depression these days, but I really thought I'd be off all my medication by this time."

I replied, "God really has done an amazing work in you, don't you think?"

She looked at me as if she knew the right answer but couldn't acknowledge it. "Well, maybe, but I still feel like a failure. No one should spend as much time asleep as I've spent over these last five years."

"But God is making progress in you, right? That's success. Give him credit."

"I'll try, but it's so hard to focus on such a little bit."

I assured her that even a little was success.

Are you downplaying God's work in your life? Give God the credit he deserves for whatever "success" he's accomplishing. It will motivate you to continue what you're doing right and also spur you to try something fresh—even if it's out of your comfort zone. It will diminish your perfectionist tendencies.

Feeling overwhelmed with unrealistic goals. How many things are on your to-do list right now? Are there more things than you have time to accomplish today, maybe even for the next week?

Many perfectionists set unattainable goals, then say, "See, I can't do anything right." We also choose to deal with the unimportant (yet often urgent) details of life, avoiding the significant projects or issues that truly make a difference, because they are harder. For instance, writers will tell you we are compelled to sharpen our pencils—all of them—when an important project needs to be started. A secretary may choose to write that insignificant letter instead of confronting her boss about his lack of integrity in dealing with her. A homemaker may vacuum instead of working on paying the bills—something that brings her great stress. We avoid whatever unpleasant task seems more difficult. Yet when we complete the important task, we have a sense of satisfaction and success. But making that decision is hard.

The antidote? Let's make a "one percent" goal to tackle that difficult project staring us in the face.

Focusing on the obstacles in the future. David Stoop writes:

> There is the tendency to look too much to the future and develop what is called the *hurdle effect*.... By looking at the future, perfectionists see only the hurdles ahead that would limit performance. Their "either-or" thinking blinds them to their past accomplishments—they choose to look only at the barriers in the future. They end up paralyzed by what they perceive to be insurmountable roadblocks.[2]

Joyce was given the assignment of recruiting new committee members for her children's school PTA and initially thought it would be fun to get involved. But each time she picked up the phone to make a call, the perfectionist's "hurdle effect" took over. "Oh, I know Hanna's schedule. She doesn't have time. Kimberly won't want to participate; she must work fifty hours a week. Cynthia has her elderly mother to care for; I can't imagine she would be interested." Joyce found a hurdle for everyone on her list and kept talking herself out of calling. She didn't realize it, but she was making decisions for those women under the guise of looking at the barriers in their lives.

Roseanne does something similar in the area of entertaining. She'd love to have several couples over for dinner but can only envision the obstacles and her possible failure. "If the roast isn't cooked right, they'll be sorry they came. I can't arrange flowers for a centerpiece like Tina does, so the decorations wouldn't be very impressive. And what if something burns? Someone might laugh at me."

Pat has her own set of hurdles in one of her lifelong desires: to be in community theater. When her local newspaper ran a notice about an audition for a play, she made plans to go and then the doubts started. "I could never learn to memorize so much, and even if I did, I'd most likely forget them on opening night. I can just imagine having everyone in the whole community snicker about a housewife like me pretending to be an actress." The day of the audition came and went, and Pat's perfectionist fear of failure prevented her from enjoying a new adventure.

As you think about a project—or even something fun you want to do—are you focused on the hurdles or the small steps you can take to accomplish it? Try to focus on the latter.

God's Definition of Failure and Success

What does God say about failure and success? We know he certainly doesn't want us to experience these tense and defeatist feelings and attitudes. Let's consider his ideas.

God forgives and forgets failure. If there was anyone in the Bible who didn't deserve to be forgiven, it was Israel's King Ahab. The Bible describes him as the most evil king Israel had ever had to that point.

> Ahab son of Omri did more evil in the eyes of the Lord than any of those before him. He not only considered it trivial to commit the sins of Jeroboam son of Nebat, but he also married Jezebel daughter of Ethbaal king of the Sidonians, and began to serve Baal and worship him. He set up an altar for Baal in the temple of Baal that he built in Samaria. Ahab also made an Asherah pole and did more to provoke the Lord, the God of Israel, to anger than did all the kings of Israel before him.
>
> 1 KINGS 16:30-33

Though he worshiped evil and was completely selfish, when he heard about the horrible way he would die, he actually repented and God responded to his humility.

> When Ahab heard these words, he tore his clothes, put on sackcloth and fasted. He lay in sackcloth and went around meekly. Then the word of the Lord came to Elijah the Tishbite: "Have you noticed how Ahab has humbled him-

self before me? Because he has humbled himself, I will not bring this disaster in his day, but I will bring it on his house in the days of his son."

1 KINGS 21:27-29

Talk about the grace of God! If God can acknowledge Ahab's repentance, then he will forgive us.

Unfortunately, we're often not listening to God's offer of forgiveness; we're paying attention to Satan's definition of failure, which never includes grace or encouragement. Billy Graham writes:

An old Scottish clergyman said the devil has two lies which he uses at two different stages. Before we commit a sin he tells us that one little sin doesn't matter; it's a trifle, and we can easily recover ourselves again. The second lie is this: after we have sinned he tells us it is hopeless, we are given over to sin and shouldn't attempt to rise. Both are total and terrible lies.

We have all fallen, and God does not consider this a trifle.... However, because Jesus Christ came and died on the cross and rose from the dead, we are not in a hopeless position. We are in a position to be reconciled to God and put back into a right relationship with Him."[3]

God doesn't look at our failures and then count us out. He says, "My daughter, you've had a temporary failure that I plan to use for your good to grow you even more. I have complete confidence in my ability to make a difference in your life. I know you *can't*, but I *can*. Trust me!"

We need to remember that when failure seems like the end

for us. It's never the end for God. He'll use it for our good and for his glory.

Obedience is success. The world defines success as accomplishment, the praise of others, power, control over others, financial wealth, and security. God's definition is one word: *obedience.* We can fail in the world's definition, but if we have obeyed God, we are a success in his eyes. He is much more concerned with *who* we are rather than what we *do.* If we can focus on God's perspective, we'll be more concerned about becoming *who* God wants us to be than accomplishing something *for* God. Whether we succeed or fail on this earth, if we've grown more like Jesus, we've reached God's goals for us.

God wants us to press on! The apostle Paul wrote,

> Not that I have already obtained all this, or have already been made perfect, but I press on to take hold of that for which Christ Jesus took hold of me. Brothers, I do not consider myself yet to have taken hold of it. But one thing I do: Forgetting what is behind and straining toward what is ahead, I press on toward the goal to win the prize for which God has called me heavenward in Christ Jesus.
>
> PHILIPPIANS 3:12-14

God says don't give up. When we perfectionists are tempted to envision and fear failure, God says, "Press on." When we think we have failed too many times, God says, "Press on." When we think we're too old to accomplish something new, God says, "Pess on." It's never too late to put aside our fear of failure and complete whatever God wants us to do: whether a project or small steps toward character development.

Failure is not an obstacle with God. We can "reach forward" until the moment we die.

Those Next Steps

Do you want to press on? Do you want to have God's definition of success? Let's look at some practical steps we can take— 1 percent at a time.

Use small amounts of time. Pick one aspect of the project facing you and do just that portion in whatever amount of time you have available *right now*—even if you can't complete it.

Notice your "absolute" words about failure. Make a conscious choice to change your comments about your mistakes and failures. Instead of saying, "I'm *always* disorganized," correct it with, "I *sometimes* become disorganized, but yesterday I cleaned out a kitchen drawer!"

Be willing to fail. It's really hard to say, "All right, even if I fail at this, I'm going to do it anyway because I believe God is telling me to do it."

Liz Curtis Higgs was willing to do exactly that and as a result, I hold in my hands the fruit of her risking. It's a book called *Mixed Signals,* her first work of adult fiction. Liz has been a successful nonfiction writer and a popular Christian speaker for many years. When she was first contemplating such a risk, she told me, "I'm about to take a leap into an abyss that I pray I can do, yet I feel called to do. Outside of the spiritual realm, I can't imagine myself going into adult fiction—romance, no less! But because God has said 'go,' I'm willing to go and possibly fail. It's more of a faith walk than I've been involved in previously."

Liz's book is getting rave reviews!

Are you willing to obey God even if it means possible failure? Do something you have avoided because you have been afraid you couldn't do it well. Here are some ideas:

- Say "yes" the next time someone asks you to make an announcement in a group setting, even though you're afraid to speak in front of people.
- Agree to give the devotional at the women's group the next time you're asked, even though you don't consider yourself spiritual enough.
- Share Christ at the next opportunity, even though you're afraid you won't be able to give a theological explanation of grace.
- Try out for the community theatre, even if you're afraid you'll forget your lines.
- Go up in a hot air balloon, even though you're afraid of heights.
- Run that 10K, even though you may have to walk some of the way.
- Take that junior college class in archeology, even though you think your brain is too old to learn.
- Take that trip by yourself since no one else has a desire, even if it means feeling a little unsafe.

As you do, you'll be thrilled that you have accomplished more than you believed possible, even if some of what you do isn't completely successful. Regardless, you're still the lovable person you've always been, the world didn't collapse around you, your friends still like you, and God still loves you! And the view from the hot air balloon is fabulous!

Distinguish between goals and desires. We may be facing failure by setting goals that are actually desires. If so, we'll be feeling like a failure constantly. I first heard the concept of the difference between goals and desires during a seminar by Dr. Neil Anderson, author of *The Bondage Breaker*. It hit a chord with me.

Goals are tangible things that can be reached and measured in a set amount of time because we have control over them. Desires are those things we would like to happen but over which we have no control.

Ask yourself which of these are goals and which are desires:

1. I want my children to grow up to love God.
2. I want to finish cleaning the bathroom by eleven this morning.
3. I want to be promoted to supervisor by August.
4. I want to set up a time to work on the Mother-Daughter Tea decorations with my cochairperson.
5. I want to read my Bible more often.
6. I want to pray for seven minutes each day.

What do you think?

The odd-numbered comments are desires: they are either vague and unmeasurable, or else they are out of your control to make happen. But the even-numbered comments are goals: they are specific (you know if you've reached them), and you have the power to cause them to happen.

Goals are the specific things we do to help make our desires possible. For instance, if we desire that our children grow up to love God, our goals could be:

- I will talk about God with my child five minutes a day by pointing out God's work around us.
- We will pray before she leaves for school, at meals, and at bedtime.
- She and I will memorize one verse of Scripture each week.
- I will bring my child to church and Sunday school.

Can you control whether those things happen? Yes. Are they specific? Yes. Therefore, they are goals. If you do those things, will you guarantee your child will grow up to love God? No. Although there's a good possibility it will happen, you can't force it to happen.

Think of the goals you've set that may be making you feel like a failure. Are they truly goals, or are they desires? Is it possible you've been feeling like a failure because you've been trying to force your desires to happen? Change your perspective. Seek God's direction for your desires, and then set reasonable and specific goals. As a result, you'll experience more success by God's definition, and you'll have courage to risk, even if you're not sure you'll do something well.

Whatever you've been procrastinating about, go do it now!

Let the story of Louise Kohr of Olympia, Washington, encourage you and illustrate how you can resist your fear of failure—regardless of the obstacles. Louise is ninety-four, yet she writes books and articles and attends writers' conferences. She has published over a thousand pieces and is currently working on her third book of object lessons. She began writing as a newspaper reporter after high school graduation, but it wasn't until age eighty-six that she sold her first children's picture book. She tells everyone, "Refuse to grow old."[4]

Adding to that, I'm telling you (and myself), let's refuse to let our perfectionist fear of failure prevent us from accomplishing what God wants us to complete.

One Step at a Time...

I know I'll never have a reader of this book say to me, "I read your book, and now I'm perfect." But I do hope I'll hear, "I read your book, and now I'm 1 percent closer to becoming excellent!" That's what this perfectionist wants to hear!

I know the Lord will work in your life because I've seen him do it in mine. Step by step, 1 percent at a time, God is working in all of us. Though at times it may seem like progress is infinitesimal, God knows how it's all adding up to make a change.

As you review what you've learned through this book, what changes can you see in your life already? Maybe one or more of these changes has already taken place:

Do you sense a little bit more that God loves you unconditionally? You don't have to earn his approval or love as much as before.

Are you relaxing more about your performance? How have you found yourself "captivating" your negative self-talk more often?

Are those absolute words becoming less frequent in your vocabulary? Can you give yourself—or others—credit for something done less than 100 percent?

Are you recognizing that life will always be a challenge, but you can relish that because you're growing closer to God? You *are* making progress, and you *are* looking a little more like Jesus every day.

Are your expectations becoming more realistic? Are you more aware of expectations that are unreasonable? Once you realize an expectation is unrealistic, do you try to adjust it? Do you notice that you can be more flexible in considering someone else's ideas or perspective?

Has it been easier to say, "Hey, that's good enough for now"? Maybe you've given yourself credit for doing the best you can, even if it doesn't measure up to your friend's accomplishments.

Maybe you've been more gracious toward someone who didn't get his or her "act" together right in front of you. Are you yelling less at the drivers on the road?

Perhaps you're not feeling so compelled to call your friend back after your phone call to explain what you meant. You know she'll love you regardless.

Did you step out and do something you've been wanting to do but have hesitated to do in the past? It doesn't have to be big—just a risk. But you did it!

See? You *are* making progress. Little by little. Step by step. God is working, and he's smiling at you, saying, "Beloved Daughter, my Princess, I know how I'm working in your life, and I'm not impatient at all. You are a delight to me, and I rejoice in your baby steps of faith and accomplishment. Do you see more of Jesus reflected in your face? I do. Do you see my glory represented to others more frequently? I know it's happening. Just press on. Don't give up. Your obedience, especially in the face of risk, gives me joy. I'm with you all the way! Keep going! I love you that much "

I'm rejoicing with you also. Let me know how you're doing. I wish you God's best.

You can reach me at:

P.O. Box 1058
Placentia, CA 92871
Kathy@larryandkathy.com
http://www.larryandkathy.com

Living With a Perfectionist

As I've spoken about perfectionism and asked people for their input, many have replied, "Be sure to write about how to live with a perfectionist." Of course they are assuming they aren't one! Here are some suggestions.

1. Don't try to change the person; instead try to understand him or her. "I'm married to a perfectionist who is critical and controlling," said Lindy. "He has high expectations of himself and others. I just let him do his thing because there is no stopping him. I let it roll off me and don't absorb it personally. I also look past my husband's behavior to his personality type plus how he was raised. I am not his mother, caretaker, or Holy Spirit that I should try to change him."

As I wrote in chapter 8, you and I cannot change anyone else. Let the Holy Spirit do that work.

2. Don't let others steal your joy; find creative ways to cope with behavior that irritates you. Barbara Johnson's husband Bill is a perfectionist. She told me:

Bill also loves trains—and he's been working on a train set for years. I didn't understand why he never finished it, but then I realized that if he ever finished it he would have to be judged by his performance, and that's not a happy thought. But if he's continually working on it, he can say it's not done yet. When I realized that about him, I could reflect that I want to get things done and over with. And even if it's not done right, I'll correct it. But my husband isn't that way.

I cope with his perfectionism by keeping the garage door down. I realized that's his area so let him handle it the way he wants. I've learned that I can't depend upon him for my joy. I have to seek my own areas of satisfaction. Don't let others steal your joy.

I love Barbara's perspective. If you can't change it, enjoy it! And if you can't change it, then work with it.

That's what Joan did. When she wanted her husband, Emmitt, to hang some pictures in their new house, he told her, "If you want that picture exactly centered over the couch, you need a yardstick, a measuring tape, and a special marker." Three weeks later, he was saying the same thing. So after she tried ten times by trial and error without the "perfect" tools, Joan found the perfect placement. She says, "Since the wall was white, I used white toothpaste to camouflage the holes in the wall. When Emmitt saw my work that night, he told me I'd done a great job and commented, 'Using the right tools really makes a difference.'" She just sweetly smiled.

Joan didn't stop there. When the white paint on their bedroom ceiling started to peel next to the air conditioning duct, Emmitt said, "We'll have to have the contractor redo the whole ceiling or it will never look right." He kissed Joan good-bye for work, and she quickly scraped off the peeling paint, found some matching paint, and redid it. She says, "That evening, Emmitt noticed the ceiling and said, 'Boy, that was quick! I didn't know you could get the contractor out that fast. He did good!' I just sweetly smiled again.' "

Joan has the right idea. Instead of getting angry over a pro-crastinating perfectionist, just do it yourself! And don't despair, because your nonperfectionist point of view does rub off. Joan says that Emmitt isn't as much of a perfectionist as he used to be. He's even commented, "After all, being imperfect does save a lot of time!"

Getting angry never solves nor helps the problem of living with a perfectionist. Instead, work with the person and you will influence him or her more than you think.

3. See others' weaknesses as opportunities for pointing them to Christ's adequacies. When we respond without anger and frus-tration to a person's perfectionist tendencies, we'll have a bet-ter opportunity of representing the Lord to them. Although they may not be open in the beginning, through patiently and gently pointing out how they might improve—without trying to force change—we may have their receptive ear.

All of us have imperfections that force us to need God, and that loved one who is the perfectionist in your life needs God's help. God can use our imperfections to create a desire for him. If you get in the way through anger or trying to force change, then that person will only become more defensive and unwill-ing to see his or her need. Your vulnerability and honesty will make them comfortable to share their doubts and stresses. Be patient, knowing God is using you even more than you realize.

See this opportunity of living with a perfectionist as a means of drawing you closer to God. You're not perfect either—so see how God wants to use this challenge in your own life. And then grow in God's grace to handle it in a godly manner.

4. Use the One Percent Principle. This is another area where the One Percent Principle can come in handy. Don't try to point out everything that's wrong in the perfectionist's life all at once. Drip on him or her instead of gushing. Don't expect huge strides. Instead, understand that change comes slowly in all of us—even when we're walking closely to the Lord.

Praise the person for small advances and sincerely see the future with hope. Share that hope with him or her. God is the God of hope, and you can infect another with it through pointing out how God has indeed caused change—even if it's small.

5. Use humor generously. Anger never creates the change we want, but humor can. By giggling instead of ridiculing, by pointing out the struggle with a smile instead of a frown, we will encourage growth.

Notice which humorous response is well received, and commit to responding in that way rather than with your own defensiveness. When anger makes it difficult to respond with humor, find the means to constructively relieve your anger through sharing with a friend, attending a support group, or asking for prayer.

⌒

Preventing Perfectionism in Your Children

Many women have asked me to write about how to prevent passing along their perfectionism to their children. Indeed, this is a concern. Here are some ideas.

1. Be sure your expectations are realistic. Corrine describes many of us when she told me, "I get on my daughter and son about things they are not completing. Then I realize later that it was not possible at that time because of their homework. Or how about this novel idea? It's because of the fact that they are only ten and five years old. I need to have more realistic expectations. I must remind myself that everybody completes things at a different pace and in their own way."

Marlene learned to do that. When her daughter told her how excited she was that she'd received a C on a test, Marlene had to bite her tongue. She explains, "I thought of other times when Sharon felt she had done well on a test and I had burst her happy bubble by suggesting she could have done better. I thought of a remark of one of my close friends that same morning. 'We rob our children of experiencing our pride in them because of our unrealistic expectations and our own false sense of pride.'

"That was it! I expected my daughter to be a top student, as I had been. Although she had been diagnosed as a borderline learning-disabled child in second grade, I had concluded that if she worked hard enough she could grow beyond her limitations.

"'You can do it,' I told her time and time again when she was feeling discouraged by her studies. Years later I was still trying to encourage her, yet unknowingly my message had changed to one that was tearing her down rather than building her up. I had failed to see my daughter's frustration as I kept insisting, 'You can do better.' I had forgotten that a C for her is like an A for someone else. I was the one who had become learning-disabled as I began to withhold my praise because she was not 'performing' to my expectations. The problem was not with Sharon but with me—with my own pride.

"The Lord sees all of my flaws and shortcomings—including the times I don't even try to reach my potential—yet in his kindness and grace he still accepts me and tells me I am his beloved child. Patiently he keeps encouraging me to grow, while at the same time he fills me with hope and confidence in what I can be through him."

In the past, Marlene had felt devastated when she realized her mistake. Now here was her chance to respond differently! She replied, "I'm really proud of you, Sharon." Marlene says, "I knew those words were the greatest gift I could give her."

At times, it's difficult to know what to expect from our children. We can read child development books, talk to other parents, take parenting classes, and pray for God's wisdom. Yet, be careful not to compare your children with other children. Each one is an individual. Gain general ideas from others, but don't ever mention another child to your own children as a means of trying to influence them to change. That will only make them feel they are not unconditionally loved, and it may cause them to try to become perfect to gain that love.

2. Recognize that although any temperament can be perfectionistic, if your child is an Analytical, it's natural. I've talked with mothers whose children at age two are already arranging things neatly in their rooms. When perfectionism appears that early, it's natural perfectionism. Many parents I talk with blame themselves for the perfectionist tendencies in their children. They try to force their children to change, often through anger or by excessive discipline. We will need to discipline them with consequences, but the consequences should be logically related to the disobedience and at the same level of seriousness.

We can prevent an overreaction by reminding ourselves that even if we could be perfect parents, our children would still be imperfect. And if their imperfection is rooted in their temperament (see chapter 8), then little we do will change it. Over time, through our influence, through maturity, and through the consequences they receive, they will change. But expecting them to immediately overcome their natural tendency toward wanting things perfect won't make a positive difference. It will only put unrealistic demands upon them.

3. Encouragement is the primary key to preventing or diminishing perfectionist tendencies in our children. Encouragement is not only a wonderful gift for anyone, it is the best motivation for people to release unrealistic expectations of themselves, others, and life. As we speak positive things about them (especially about them to others), they will sense our unconditional love and be more willing to see the good within themselves.

We've all heard, "Love the sinner and hate the sin." We will need to point out the poor decisions our children make. We will need to give consequences for their mistakes and disobedience, but we can still say, "I love you." Never withhold an expression of love as a means of trying to change or punish them. That's conditional love, which will only make them sense they must perform perfectly in order to earn your love. Instead, always affirm how much you love your children even when disciplining them or pointing out their mistakes. Then they will have a deeper sense that your love will never end—no matter what they do.

Notes

ONE
Are You a Perfectionist?

1. David Stoop, *Living With a Perfectionist* (Nashville, Tenn: Nelson, 1987), Preface. Used by permission.
2. David Seamands, *Healing for Damaged Emotions* (Wheaton, Ill.: Victor, 1981), 90.
3. Wayne Coffey, "Is It Worth It to Be Perfect?" *Seventeen*, November 1984, 183.
4. For more information, consult books such as the titles listed in these endnotes.
5. Kevin Leman, *Measuring Up* (Grand Rapids, Mich.: Revell, 1988), 94.
6. Leman, 50–51.

TWO
Most of the Time I Sense God Is Disappointed With Me

1. Charles Swindoll, *Grace Awakening* (Dallas, Tex.: Word, 1990), 8.

FOUR
I Think in Terms of "All or Nothing"

1. Stoop, 32–33. Used by permission.
2. Kevin Leman, *Bonkers* (Grand Rapids, Mich.: Revell, 1987), 123–24.
3. David A Seamands, *Healing Grace* (Wheaton, Ill.: Victor, 1988), 20.

FIVE
I Should Have My Act Together by Now

1. Swindoll, 204.
2. Swindoll, 204.
3. W.E. Vine, *Vine's Expository Dictionary of Old and New Testament Words* (Old Tappan, N.J.: Revell, 1981), 138.
4. Max Lucado, *On the Anvil* (Wheaton, Ill.: Tyndale, 1985) 45–46. All rights reserved. Used by permission.

SIX
My Expectations Tend to Be Unrealistic

1. Lee Ezell, *Porcupine People* (Ann Arbor, Mich.: Servant, 1998), 145.
2. Chuck Lynch, *I Should Forgive, But...* (Nashville, Tenn.: Word, 1998), 34.
3. Elisabeth Elliot, *Love Has a Price Tag* (Ann Arbor, Mich.: Servant, 1979), 97.

SEVEN
"Good" Is Rarely "Good Enough"

1. Kevin Leman, *The Pleasers: Women Who Can't Say No and the Men Who Control Them* (Old Tappan, N.J.: Revell, 1987), 158.
2. Original source unknown; sent to me via Email.

EIGHT
Why Can't People Get Their Act Together?

1. Stoop, 56. Used by permission.
2. Kathy Collard Miller and D. Larry Miller, adapted from *When the Honeymoon's Over* (Wheaton, Ill.: Shaw, 1997), 19–20. Used by permission.
3. Seamands, *Healing Grace*, 26.

NINE
I'm Compelled to Straighten Out Misunderstandings

1. Stoop, 35. Used by permission.
2. Leman, *Measuring Up*, 194.
3. Billy Graham, "What Ten Years Have Taught Me," *Christian Century,* February 17, 1960, 186.

TEN
I Won't Begin Something If I Can't Do It Well

1. David Burns, "The Perfectionist's Script for Self-Defeat," *Psychology Today,* November 1980, 36–37.
2. Stoop, 34. Used by permission.
3. Billy Graham, *Till Armageddon* (Waco, Tex.: Word, 1981), 59–60.
4. Niki Anderson, "A Profile of Inspirational Writer Louise Kohr," *The Christian Communicator,* January 1998, 3.

Books by Kathy Collard Miller